Logic Pro

Tips and Tricks

Stephen Bennett

PC Publishing

PC Publishing
Keeper's House
Merton
Thetford
Norfolk IP25 6QH
UK

Tel +44 (0)1953 889900
email info@pc-publishing.com
website http://www.pc-publishing.com

First published 2010

ISBN 13: 978 1906005 153

British Library Cataloguing in Publication Data
A catalogue record for this book is available from the British Library

Printed and bound in Great Britain by Jellyfish Solutions, Hants

Contents

Preface

Apple's Logic audio sequencer program is highly renowned for its flexibility and customisable nature. Like any complex piece of software, the means to achieving a given goal is not always obvious – a problem compounded by Logic's ability to perform most functions in several different ways. Occasionally, Logic's features are obscure and poorly documented – Sometimes; they are not even documented at all! All this doesn't help with workflow one bit. With Logic you could be recording audio, Virtual instruments and MIDI instruments. You'll be using virtual effects plug-ins and, perhaps, external classic hardware effects units. You'll be automating volume, pan and all the parameters of your plug-ins. You'll be musician, recording engineer, producer, mixing and mastering engineer all in one. The sheer complexity of the software means that many useful functions are hidden from view, often deep in nested menus or obscure Key Commands.

The book is divided into Chapters covering most of Logic's areas – but don't regard this as a book that's only useful when you want to look up a particular way of working. Dip into it, keep it by the bed or read it while having breakfast. You'll stumble across new ways of working and Key Commands that you didn't know existed. While writing the book the author was heard to exclaim on more than one occasion 'Well – I never knew that!' Many of the tips apply to several different areas of Logic, whereas others are specific to one window or editor. All are useful to the Logic user. The book mainly covers Logic Studio 9 but also has many useful tips for the pre-Logic 8 user as, although Apple have changed much of the visual look of the program, most of the functionality remains 'under the hood'.

Over many years of use, the author has searched out useful tips and tricks to help get the most from Logic. This book is the results of many hours of puzzled frowns, bitten nails and years of research. Read the book from cover to cover or dip into individual sections – whichever way you use the book will improve your workflow and increase your productivity, and pleasure, when using this powerful and fascinating piece of software.

Acknowledgments

I'd like to thank the following for their invaluable help in preparing this book. The on-line Logic community, Phil Chapman at PC Publishing, Christine Wilhelmy at Apple, Mike Senior, Andy Jones, Debbie Poyser and Nell McLeod for the support, help and advice without which I'd still be scratching my head and shouting, to no-one in particular, 'why doesn't that work the way it should?'

This book is dedicated to my Parents William and Mary.

Setting up and optimization

The first problem that users new to Logic Pro have to solve is usually one of set-up. Getting audio into and out of the program can, at first, cause much head scratching. After you've got the Audio working, you'll need to sort out MIDI and the puzzle begins once more. This chapter contains tips and tricks that can get you up and running with Logic as soon as you have everything connected and switched on. It may seem obvious, but before you try any of the tips in this chapter, make sure you have connected all the leads correctly and powered on all your equipment. If I had a Euro for every time I've solved a problem by switching on an Interface or plugging in a USB lead I wouldn't need to write this book! It also pays to read the, usually short, manuals that come with any third-party Audio or MIDI interfaces to make sure everything is set-up OK.

Which OS?

Which OS (Operating System)? Although some users are still using MacOS OS9 or earlier, these days the majority will be using a variant of OSX. Which version you use depends on your Mac and which version of Logic you are using – though versions 10.2 ('Jaguar') onwards provide the CoreAudio and CoreMIDI protocols essential for working with Logic. Occasionally, a version of Logic will force an upgrade of the OS, though many users prefer to leave the upgrades until absolutely necessary. This 'if it 'ain't broke, don't fix it' approach has some merits – you'll nearly always have less problems when you are not at the cutting edge of technological advances. Also be aware that any third-party plug-ins will also usually need upgrading when you change the OS. If in doubt, keep an eye on the manufacture's website.

32 or 64 bit? Logic 9.1 is the first version of Logic able to run in both 32 and 64 bit mode. 64 bit operation allows Logic to access more than 4GB or RAM which should remove any 'out of memory' error messages when using memory intensive plug-ins. Plug-ins optimized for 64 bit operation will open as normal – however, legacy 32 bit ones open in a separate window (the 32 bit Audio Unit Bridge) and have some limitations on usage. Eventually, most third – party plug-ins will be ported to 64 bit – check the manufacturer's websites for details. Logic can be opened in 64 bit mode by right or CTRL clicking on the Logic application in the /Applications folder and de-selecting the 32 bit mode checkbox. Note that Logic can run in 64 bit mode while OSX itself is still in its default 32 bit mode – which it needs to be if any of your drivers for audio and MIDI gear are 32 bit – only.

Drivers

CoreAudio and CoreMIDI, Apple's Operating System (OS) level software is the 'glue' that binds together Logic and any third-party Audio or MIDI gear you have. The third-party company provides a software CoreAudio or

CoreMIDI driver that communicates with the Macintosh's OS. All Logic has to do is to use these drivers to use the connected Audio and MIDI hardware. It's important that you use the correct drivers; otherwise you may have problems right away.

Use the correct driver for the correct version of the OS and Logic

Once you've installed the drivers, you should visit the hardware vendor's website right away and download the latest and/or correct versions of the driver. Each version of Logic and/or the OS can need different drivers.

Check that the drivers are loaded correctly

OSX has a program, Audio MIDI Setup, which is where you'll see the CoreAudio and CoreMIDI drivers you have installed on your Mac. If you run this program and check everything is OK, Logic will be able to find the correct drivers when it loads. This will avoid a lot of grief later on.

Figure 1.1
Run Audio MIDI Setup and check everything is OK.

Audio and your system's beeps and bells

You may want to set the System output to 'Built-in audio'. This will make sure that Operating system warnings will not be played through your audio interface.

MIDI

If you connect your audio interface and plug in all your MIDI gear (if you have any) you can use the Rescan MIDI button to get all of your equipment displayed in the MIDI devices window. You can see your MIDI interfaces and the Ports the MIDI gear is connected to. If the automatic detection doesn't suc-

Figure 1.2
In the MIDI devices window you can see your MIDI interfaces and the Ports the MIDI gear is connected to.

Figure 1.3
Using the 'Add device' button you can rename an external device.

Tip

Don't move the Logic application from the Applications folder otherwise System Update won't be able to find it. If you need a copy elsewhere, hold down the control key and click on the Logic program file (or right-click on it) to make an Alias and drag this to the location you desire.

ceed, you can manually add devices using the 'Add device' button. You can then rename the external device ('Yamaha DX7') and drag the virtual cables as shown in Figure 1.3.

Keeping up to date

You should run OSX's Software Update (when connected to the Internet) regularly to check for Logic and other system updates. It's also a good idea to go to the website of your Audio, MIDI and Controller hardware manufacturers on a regular basis to see if there are any updates available.

The 'other' book

Logic's manuals are available from the programs Help menu. PDF manuals are also available from www.apple.com.

Operating system optimization

Apple's OSX is a version of the UNIX operating system. There are a few main-tenance tasks that you should perform on a regular basis. If you do these, you're less likely to have software or disk access problems – both are impor-tant when using Logic.

Repairing permissions

As OSX is a relatively secure OS and you can have several different users. OSX keeps track of who can have access to files by setting permissions on files and disks. These permissions can get corrupted and cause various prob-lems. You may have problems installing software or strange disk-based errors may occur – such as Logic not being able to access audio files. You should repair permissions often – at least once a week. Here's how you do it.

- Run the Disk Utility program from the /Applications/Utilities folder
- Select a disk
- Click on 'Repair disk permissions'

Figure 1.5
Run the Disk Utility program regularly.

You'll see a progress bar appear and any permissions problems will be fixed.

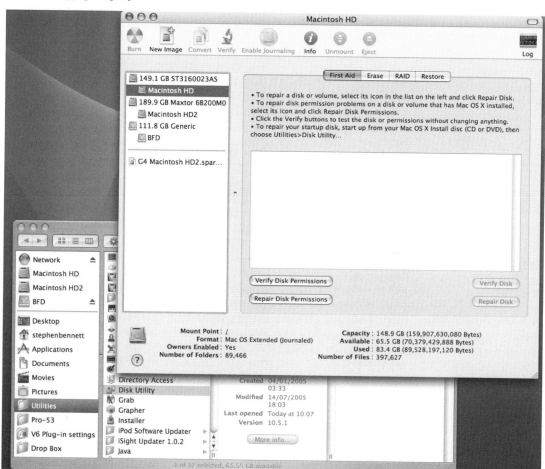

Maintenance scripts

In daily use, OSX stores a lot of information in temporary files. If you leave your Mac on all the time, small shell scripts, called 'maintenance tasks', run automatically daily, weekly and monthly to delete these logs and other temporary files. You can regain a lot of disk space running these files if you haven't done them for a long time. Here's how you do it. Run the Terminal from the /Applications/Utilities folder.

Figure 1.6

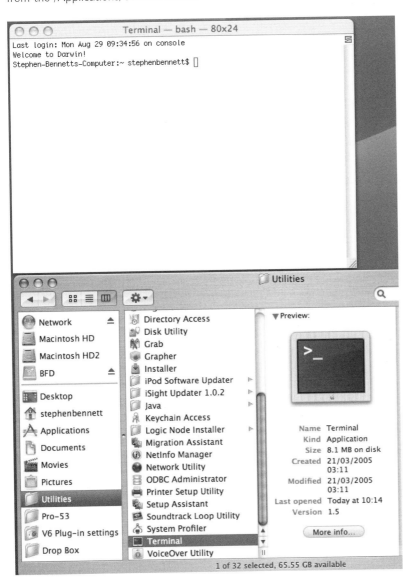

The daily script

Type 'sudo sh /etc/daily' (without the quotes)
Enter your administrator password.
The script will run.

The weekly script

Type 'sudo sh /etc/weekly (without the quotes)
Enter your administrator password.
The script will run – it will take longer than the daily script.

The monthly script

Type 'sudo sh /etc/monthly (without the quotes)
Enter your administrator password.
The script will run – it will take longer than the monthly script.

Aggregate devices

Logic (under OSX 10.4 or later) can use Aggregate devices. These are a group of two or more Audio and/or MIDI interfaces that appear to Logic as though they were one combined device.

Aggregate devices are created in the Audio MIDI setup program detailed earlier in the chapter. Open the program and run the Audio>Aggregate devices editor.

Figure 1.7

Figure 1.8

Figure 1.9

You'll see a list of all connected and installed devices. Select the ones you wish to use. Rename the device (Figure 1.8).

You'll see that this new aggregate device ('MOTU/Photon') has 12 inputs and outputs – The MOTU has 10, the Alesis Photon 2. Close the editor window. You can now choose this device in Logic's Audio menu>Audio hardware and drivers window. (Figure 1.9). Use the highest quality interface as the master clock

Speeding up Logic
Depending on the power of your computer and its Video card, you may want to try these tips to improve the performance of your system.

Turn off Airport and Bluetooth
They both use processing power better directed towards plug-ins.

Close all unnecessary programs and Widgets
Logic uses a lot of memory and programs running in the background eat up precious RAM.

Disable all anti Virus software
This type of software is constantly checking the hard drive, thus reducing the amount of bandwidth available for recording.

AU (Audio Unit) Manager
When you first run Logic, it checks that any third party AU plug-ins pass the stringent AU validation criteria set out by Apple. If they all pass, Logic will boot normally. However, if they fail, Logic will disable the AU plug-ins. If this happens, you should check with the plug-in company whether there is a 'Logic 7 or later' version and install that.

You can, however, allow failed plug-ins to be used in Logic. Be aware though that you do this at your own risk; unstable plug-ins can cause Logic to crash.

Enabling plug-ins that have failed the AU validation
- Start the Logic AU Manager from the Preferences>Start Logic AU Manager menu item.
- The AU manager loads.
- Enable failed AU plug-ins by clicking on the Use check box (Figure 1.10).

When you have enabled all the plug-ins you want, click on OK. Logic will reload and the new AU plug-ins will be available in the usual way.

Figure 1.10

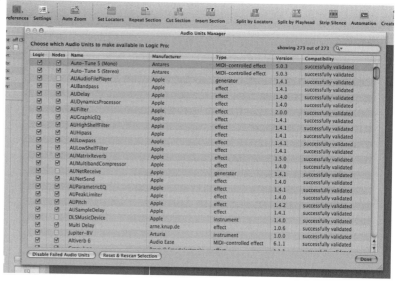

Other hardware

Hard drives

It's useful to have a second fast (7200rpm or greater) hard drive to store all your audio and Logic Song files on. Not only does this make backing up easier, but also it separates the throughput of data to disk from the OS and EXS24 sample loading. This extra drive could be internal to the Mac or it could be an external Firewire (400 or 800) or USB 2.x drive. USB 1.x is too slow for audio recording.

Which audio interface?

Although there are a lot of different kinds of audio interface on the market, these can be broken down into a few groupings which should help you decide which is right for your needs. The main issues are Number of Inputs, number of outputs, USB, Firewire or PCI.

Number of inputs

The more inputs you have, the more audio signals you can feed into Logic.

- You need only two inputs if you only want to record a mono or stereo signal.
- You'll need more inputs if you want to record a whole band, drums or return the signal from several hardware effects units, such as reverbs and compressors, back into Logic.
- You'll need more outputs if you want to produce a surround sound output (5:1 needs 6 outputs), you need to send signals to several hardware effects units or need to set up complex monitor mixes for band members (8 outputs can produce 8 different monitor mixes if you use a separate send per output.)

Firewire or USB 2.0 connection

These high-speed interfaces are useful if you need portability. They can often be powered from the computer so you don't need a separate power supply unit. This is especially useful for Laptop users.

These usually are equipped with 2-8 analog outputs plus they often have 2-8 digital outputs.

PCI Interfaces

These fit on an internal card in the Mac – so they are not suitable for Laptops or any other Macs without PCI cards. They often can support many more outputs and inputs – 24 is not uncommon.

Using the Mac's internal sound

You can choose to use the Mac's internal sound card. You select it in the Audio hardware and drivers window (from the main Audio menu) (Figure 1.11).

The quality of the inputs on the Mac is not as good as a third-party interface (and not all Macs have them anyway), but the output is adequate for monitoring, If you are bouncing down mixes to disk in Logic, you won't need any extra outputs. You can also use the digital audio interface on some Macs to send a signal to a digital to analog converter. You'll also find that you usually can't get the lowest buffer size using the internal sound facilities.

Tip

You can often increase the number of ins and outs by using an 8-channel analog to digital expander box and plug it into the ADAT socket of the interface. These extra ins and outs appear in Logic as one combined set.

Info

Interfaces often have monitor sections, latency free monitors, headphone outputs and DSP plugins onboard that can be used in Logic.

Figure 1.11

Templates, Projects and back-ups

The 'basic' format of a saved Logic session is called a Project (Figure 2.1). A Project is a collection of Logic Song and all associated files ('*Assets*') collected together into a single folder and sub-folders. Apart from the usefulness of col-

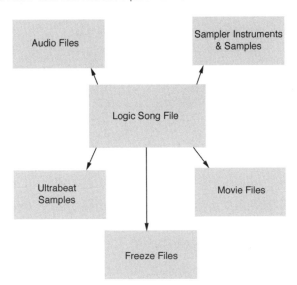

Figure 2.1

lecting all of Logic's files together in one place when backing-up, it's also useful to do this when you want to send a Logic song to collaborators. A Project is created when you use the Save function in the File menu (Figure 2.2).

Figure 2.2

Tip

If you just want to save a Project as a different version without duplicating all the assets, deselect the Include Assets tickbox. This just then saves a basic song file.

If you click on the Include Assets and the little arrow next to the Advanced Options text you can choose which associated files to save (or collect) into a Logic Project folder. Which you choose depends on what you want to do with the Song.

If you want to work with this song only on the Macintosh it was recorded on or another Macintosh which has the same samples loaded running the same version of Logic

In this case, you'd probably only want to Include copy external audio files to project folder and, if you are using them, any Movie files. Samples, EXS Instruments and Impulse responses (for Space Designer) can be left in their default folders.

If you want to work with this song on another system where you can't be sure it has the same version of Logic and associated samples

In this case, you'd want to copy everything to the Project folder.

Saving backups

To make sure you don't lose an important previous version of your Song, You can set Logic to save up to 100 backups in the Project folder. This is set from the Preferences>General menu.

Audio file housekeeping

During a recording session, you'll accumulate lots of audio that won't be used in the final mix. All these files are displayed in the bin tab of the Media inspector (which replaces the Audio window in earlier Logic versions than 8). All these audio files take up hard disk space. Logic has various features that

Figure 2.3

can help out. You'll need to select the Bin tab from the media inspector (Figure 2.3). Most of these functions work when you've selected an audio file or Region in the Bin.

The bin Audio File menu

Optimize File(s) This will delete any fragments of any selected audio files not used the Arrange page.

Delete Files(s) This deletes any selected files. See the section below on the Edit window for selection criteria.

The bin Edit window

There are various selection criteria in this menu to help you find files not being used in a Particular Song.

Select Unused Use this function to select all files NOT being used in the Project.

*Select files...*this function has a sub-menu which allows you to use various criteria for selecting files. These will help you make sure you don't delete files used in other Projects. (Figure 2.4).

Tip

You can use the bin to rename audio recordings and files to more useful names than the default ones Logic gives them. Just click and hold on the recording's name.

Figure 2.4

Tip

You can find any selected Regions that contain audio files in the Finder using the Arrange Page > Audio > Show selected audio files in Finder.

Templates

Logic can store user-defined Projects as 'Templates'. You may, for example, have a template that you use for multi-track recording, one for stereo recording, one for general use, one for mastering and so on. Templates are just normal Logic Projects which are stored in a specific location and can be recalled at will.

Your own defined Templates are stored in the Users/Library/Application Support/Logic/Project Templates folder.

Saving Templates

Create a Logic Song you want to use as a Template. In the example below, the Template has been set-up for recording 16 audio inputs. Each Logic Projects can have it's own Screensets.   Once the Project has been created and modified to your satisfaction, save it from the File>Save as Template menu item (Figure 2.5).

Figure 2.5 (left)

Figure 2.6 (right)

Loading Templates

Select the File>New menu item. You can now select a Template from the 'Template' boxes. Notice that there's a 'My templates' folder where your own custom Templates are stored (Figure 2.6).

Modifying Templates

Load in a Template, modify it and save it as described above.

Tip

You can create sub-folders in the Users/Library/Application Support/Logic/Project Template folder to keep similar Templates grouped together.

Getting around in Logic

There are many ways to perform tasks in Logic, which can, at first, seem daunting. However, as this is part of the program's highly customisable personality, it means you can usually work in any way you want. If a particular way of working offends, then change it! This chapter covers tips on getting around Logic's functions and should help you to improve workflow.

Toolbox

You can set up two assignable Tools per Screenset by selecting them from the pull down menus on the top right of the Arrange page (Figure 3.1). Then when you press the Apple key, the mouse cursor will change to the second pre-selected tool.

If you have a mouse with a right mouse button you can assign it to open the Toolbox at the cursor position from the Preferences>Global>Editing> Open Toolbox menu item.

If you set the Preferences>Global parameter to 'Is assignable to a tool' and you have a mouse with a right mouse button, you can store three assignable tools per Screenset. The first is the tool you select by left clicking on the Toolbox. The second you set up by Apple-clicking on the Tool you require. Clicking on the required tool on the Toolbox with the right mouse key chooses the third.

Figure 3.1

Scrolling with the mouse

The scroll wheel can be used for scrolling up and down in a window. Holding down the Alt key while you do this zooms the tracks vertically, whilst holding down the Apple key scrolls along the Song's timeline. Holding down the Shift and Alt keys while scrolling, zooms the window horizontally.

If you hold down the Control and Shift key in a Window, the cursor becomes a 4-pointed arrow. You can now scroll around the window in both horizontal and vertical directions.

Links

To make sure all open windows are showing the same data, you need to make sure the Link icon is 'ON' for all windows. Logic's link feature can seem a little complicated – there are basically two modes of operation.

Tip

Pressing ESC will always bring up the Toolbox at the cursor point. If you press ESC then the relevant number or letter key, a tool is selected. For example, pressing ESC then 2 selects the Pencil tool in the Arrange page. Pressing ESC twice always reverts to the Arrow tool.

Tip

With a suitable Macintosh, you can use two fingers as a scroll tool on a track pad.

Figure 3.2

Link mode (Same level link)

If you click once on the Link Icon, the window always displays the same contents as the top window, if that is possible. Here's an example of what this means.

If you have an Event editor and an Arrange page open, and the Link icon is ON (purple) – by clicking on it once or right-or CTRL clicking on it and selecting Same Level Link.

Then clicking on a Region on the Arrange page will show the following Event editor window. Note that the Event editor shows the same 'level' of data as the Arrange page – i.e. Regions.

Figure 3.3

Figure 3.4

Now click on a note in the Piano roll editor. You will see the Event list editor will change to show the same notes as those shown the Piano roll editor, i.e. it is at the same 'level' of data as the Piano roll window (Figure 3.5).

Link – (Contents link)

If you double click on the Link icon (right- or CTRL-clicking on it and selecting Content link – the icon turns yellow) the behaviour of the windows changes. If you have the same Piano roll editor, Event editor and Arrange page open and the Link icon is yellow, clicking on the Arrange page will show the following Event editor window (Figure 3.6).

Figure 3.5

Figure 3.6

Note that the Event editor shows data one 'level' below that of the Arrange page, i.e. the note data of the selected region in the Arrange page. Now click on a note in the Piano roll editor. You will see the Event list editor will keep the same data as the Piano roll editor. You cannot have one 'level' below that of MIDI events!

If you switch on both the Content catch icon (the little 'running man') and the Link icon in 'Contents link' you can force the editors to display the notes of each region currently being played on a selected track as the song position line passes over it.

Tip

If you want the Editors to show the notes within a Region as the Song position passes over that Region, make sure the Content catch is ON (see below) and The Link icon is in Contents link mode.

Linking and the Environment

If you click once on the Link icon in the Environment, selecting an instrument in the Arrange window will select that instrument object in the Environment even if it has to change layers to do it. This is useful if you select a modifier, such as an arpeggiator in the Arrange page, and you want to change its parameters from the Environment's Parameter box. You can have many windows open with different Link Settings saved as a Screenset.

Catch mode (Running man) – making sure all your open windows are synchronized

To make sure all the open windows are showing the same section of the Song, make sure the Running man icon is 'ON'

Info

In Logic Pro 8 or later it's no longer possible to open an independent Editor window when you double-click on a Region. You can however select a Region and open the window of your choice using the respective Key commands that open the individual Editors.

Setting a default editor

Depending on the way you work, you may want the Piano Roll, List edit or Score editor tabbed window to open when you double click on a Region. You set this in the Global Preferences Editing window.

Easy dragging

It's easy to accidentally drag Regions or notes vertically instead of horizontally or vice versa in the Arrange, Piano roll and Score editors. To stop this happening, you can limit scrolling to one direction only from the Global>Editing preferences window. Hold down the Shift key while dragging to disable this limitation.

Playing music from the computer keyboard

If you don't have a MIDI or other controller music keyboard handy, you can use the computer keyboard. You can set the Caps Lock Key to show the on-screen keyboard from the Global Preferences Caps Lock Key window.

Key Commands

Key Commands are one of Logic's most important features – however, because some of them are often poorly documented they are not always used to the full. It's important to realise that some functions in Logic are available *only* via Key Commands. Open the Key Commands window from the Logic Pro>Preferences menu (Figure 3.8).

Logic functions which are only available as Key Commands

These have a 'dot' next to them in the Key Commands window (Figure 3.9).

Finding which Key Command is assigned to which computer key

Make sure 'Learn by Key label' and 'Learn by Key Position' are not selected. When you press a key on the computer keyboard, the Key Command it's been assigned to will be highlighted (Figure 3.10).

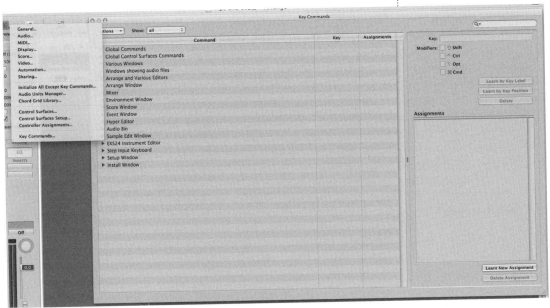

Figure 3.8
The Key Commands window

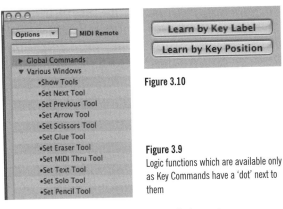

Figure 3.10

Figure 3.9
Logic functions which are available only
as Key Commands have a 'dot' next to
them

Assigning Key Commands to the numeric keypad

Click on the 'Learn by key position' button and select the key Command you
wish to assign. You'll see that the ASCII code for the key is displayed.

Figure 3.11 (left)

Figure 3.12 (below)

Key Commands template

You can copy all your Key Commands into a text editor and print them out.
Use the Key Commands Options Pull down menu, Copy key Commands to
Clipboard item (Figure 3.12).

Info

You can also import Key Commands using the general import feature – see Chapter 6.

Importing Key Commands

From the same menu, you can import Key Commands from a Logic preferences file such as the version 7 one in /Library/Preferences/Logic/com.apple. logic.pro

Undo and Redo

Most procedures in Logic can be Undone. The number of Edit>Undo steps is defined In the Global preferences window. Note that the greater the number of Undo steps you define the greater the memory used to store these steps. The Edit>UNDO history window allows you to undo edits back to a specific point and redo them gain if you're not happy with the results. Not all of Logic's functions can be undone; though Logic will usually warn you if this is so.

Markers

Markers are very useful for defining various sections of a Song. You can place a Marker at the choruses, verses, bridges and so on. Markers can also contain text information – each Marker has a little word processor, where you can type in helpful information. You may want to remember how a guitar was recorded, how a vocal take was done, what settings you used on a non programmable hardware box and so on.

Markers are most easily created and manipulated using Global Tracks. Make sure you can see these by making sure they are selected from the Arrange page's View menu>Global Tracks item. You can choose which Global Tracks are displayed from the Configure Global Tracks menu or right or CTRL clicking on the Global Tracks in the Track list – make sure the 'Marker' parameter is checked (Figure 3.13).

Figure 3.13

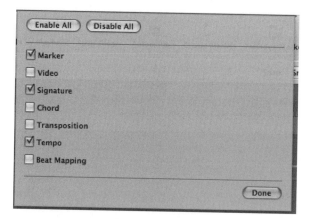

Enable All   Disable All

- ☑ Marker
- ☐ Video
- ☑ Signature
- ☐ Chord
- ☐ Transposition
- ☑ Tempo
- ☐ Beat Mapping

Done

Tip

Use the set of Marker Key Commands to create, move around to and open the Marker List.

Markers can be created by highlighting a Region and clicking on the 'From Regions' button, by CTRL or Right clicking on the Marker lane in the Global Track or from the Options>Marker menu items (Figure 3.14).

Once you have created your Markers you can edit them. Open the marker list from the Option>Marker menu item (Figure 3.15). Here you can edit the start point of each Marker directly by double clicking on the Position field. You can define how the Position is displayed from the View menu you may want it in Bars (Figure 3.16) or SMPTE units (Figure 3.17).

Figure 3.14
Markers can be created by highlighting a Region and clicking on the 'From Regions' button or from the Options>Marker menu items.

Figure 3.15
Open the marker list from the Option>Marker menu item.

Figure 3.16

Figure 3.17

Double clicking on a Marker opens a text editor window (Figure 3.18). Here you can edit the Marker text. As you can see the Marker window is a small text editor. You can change the font and text size.

Figure 3.18

Figure 3.19

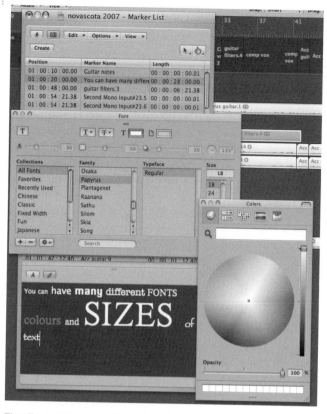

The Font (A) menu allows you to change various Text parameters and the text colours (Figure 3.19).

If the Running man icon is highlighted and the Marker window is open, the text in the Marker window will change as the Song progresses (and the Markers change) (Figure 3.20).

Figure 3.20

- Use the Key Commands 'Set Locators By Previous Marker' and 'Set Locators By Next Marker' and 'Enable Cycle' to quickly move through a Song. If Logic is playing when you use these Key Commands, the Playhead (SPL) will move to the new Marker and cycle round the Locators.

- Drag a marker down towards the Arrange page region area to delete it.
- Drag the cycle region to the Marker area to create a Marker the length of the cycle region (Figure 3.21).

Figure 3.21

Groups in the Media browser's bin

In a complex song, you may have hundreds of audio files in the Audio bin. This can make tracking down individually files a nightmare. Fortunately, you can sort audio files into groups, just like folders in OSX. Use the menu item View>Create Group. You'll be asked to name the group.

Figure 3.22

Figure 3.23

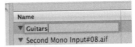

You can then drag audio Regions from the bin into the Group (Figure 3.24).

Figure 3.24

Tip

You can also Group files using various criteria – these are chosen from the View>Group files by menu item.So, for example if you select Regions in the Arrange page, you can add them to a Group using the Group file by selection in Arrange menu item.

You can see the files within the group by clicking on the triangle to the left of the Group name.

Figure 3.25

Creating Tracks and Objects

Figure 3.26

You can create Tracks and Objects in the Arrange page from the Track Create icons (Figure 3.26).

Clicking on the '+'opens a window where you can create as many tracks as you want of whatever type in mono or stereo. You can select which Inputs and Outputs the Tracks are set to and in which order they are loaded onto the Arrange page.

Figure 3.27

Clicking on these places them in the Arrange page and the Environment. The Open Library tick box opens the Library in the Media browser ready for you to select a Channel strip (Figure 3.27).

The icon to the right of the '+' creates a duplicate of the selected Track.

Info

Double clicking on the space under the last Track on the Arrange page will also create a new Track.

Snapping and Dragging

When moving Regions around the Arrange page or notes in the Piano roll editor the way they butt up against each other is determined by the settings of the Snap and Drag pull down menus at the top right of the respective pages (Figure 3.28).

Figure 3.28

Snap menu

Using this menu (Figure 3.29) you can determine the behaviour of the drag.

- Smart – this will usually allow you to drag a region where you need to. You can always make the movement finer using the modifier keys described above.
- Bar – this limits the dragging to individual bars.
- Beat - this limits the dragging to individual beats.
- Division - this limits the dragging to Divisions (as set in the Time signature)
- Format – if you have the View>SMPTE Time ruler switched on, you can drag and snap to using the SMPTE values.
- You can also snap to individual samples, ticks, frames and quarter frames (QF)
- You can snap Automation too, but if you're finding that you're getting problems having Automation start at the same time as other MIDI data you can also add an Automation offset.

Figure 3.29

Drag menu

The Drag menu (Figure 3.30) defines how regions butt up to regions they are dragged against.

- Overlap – this mode preserves the region size when dragged – even if overlapping another region (Figures 3.31 and 3.32).

Figure 3.30

Figures 3.31 and
Figure 3.32

- No Overlap – if you drag a region over another region using this mode, the second region is truncated in size (Figures 3.33 and 3.34).

Figures 3.33 and
Figure 3.34

- X-fade – this mode automatically cross-fades two adjacent regions. It's useful if you want to remove clicks from the transition. You can also use the crossfade tool for more complex fades.
- Shuffle L and Shuffle R – these two modes will automatically butt up a dragged region to the left and right respectively of another region.

Moving, copying, cutting, deleting and resizing regions

Moving, copying and resizing are all done on an invisible grid set by the bar and beat settings in the Transport bar (left). You can change how fine this grid is holding down the following modifier keys while performing the required function.

CTRL   Moves in ticks
CTRL + SHIFT   No Grid. Movement is unrestrained

Nudging Regions and notes.

There's a whole series of nudge event Key Commands for moving Regions and note events very precisely. They allow you to choose the type of the nudge – for example, SMPTE time and beat, bar and Tick (Figure 3.35).

Figure 3.35

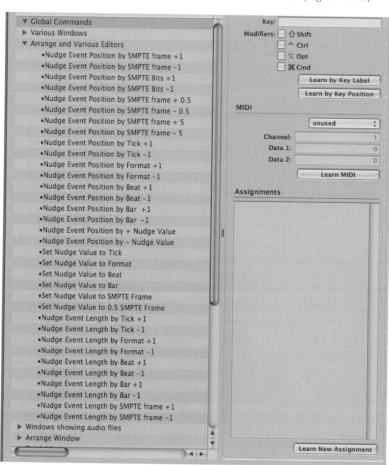

Screensets

These are one of Logic's most famous features. While the single window Arrange page introduced in Logic 8 simplifies the program's use, Screensets are essential for making the most of the multi-window approach of the program, especially if you have multiple monitors or a small screen. Screensets are stored with along with a Project and you can copy Screensets between Projects using the Project settings Import settings menu item (Figure 3.36). This opens a window where you can choose what to import and the Song you wish to Import from (Figure 3.37).

Figure 3.36

Figure 3.37

If you are used to using the numeric keys to change Screensets, you must define these specifically in the Key Commands window in Logic Pro 9. To select Screensets with numbers over 10, hold down the Control key and type in the required number (Figure 3.38).

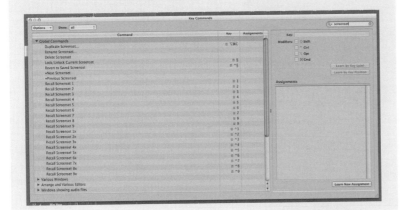

Tip

You can Lock Screensets from the Windows>Screenset> Lock Screenset menu.

You can select your Screensets from the Windows>Screenset menu (Figure 3.39).

Screensets can be copied from the Windows>Screenset>Copy   Screenset menu. In Logic Pro 9 you can also give Screensets useful names and duplicate them.

Figure 3.39

Useful Key Commands for Screensets

- Next/Previous key Command – sometimes it's quicker to move around the different Screensets using this Key Command.
- You can Lock, Copy and Paste Screensets using the respective Key Commands.
- Revert to Current Screenset – if you have moved things around in an unlocked Screenset, this Key Command brings the Screenset back to the way it was when you first selected it.

Figure 3.40

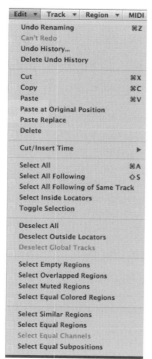

Selecting things

Most of Logic's windows have several options for selecting items in their Edit menus. These make it easy to select, for example, muted objects or all Regions following the Playhead (SPL) (Figure 3.40). Most of these select options have corresponding Key Commands.

Marquee tool

This tool (Figure 3.41) is especially useful for selecting parts of Regions. If you choose the tool and draw the tool in a rectangle across a Region, it will be selected (Figure 3.42).

Figure 3.41

Figure 3.42 (left) and Figure 3.43 (above)

Once selected, you can use the Arrow tool to drag the selected Region, hold down the Option Key and copy it, Mute it or perform any of the regular Region editing commands (Figure 3.43). You can also use the Crop Regions outside Marquee Selection Key Command to split the Region.

All of the following assume the Marquee Tool is active.

- Double clicking on a Region splits it
- Once you've highlighted a part of a Region with the Marquee Tool, right or CTRL clicking on the selection splits the Region at the boundaries of the selection.
- Clicking on the background on the Arrange page and pressing play, plays from that point.
- Dragging an area on a Region will play just that area
- Dragging an area with Automation on will create 4 Automation nodes when using the Arrow tool.

Snap to Transient

In Logic Pro 9, you can use the Key Commands relating to the Snap to Transient feature of the Marquee tool to edit audio Regions 'on the beat' (Figure 3.44).

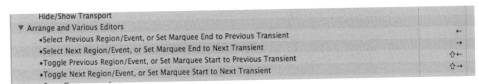

Figure 3.44

Selecting windows without bringing them to the front

You can select objects in any background window without bringing that window to the front. You need to click and hold the mouse to stop the window becoming the focus.

Copying between Songs

Logic can open many Projects at the same time and Regions can be freely copied between each Song. To do this, Load each Project into Logic (Figure 3.45).

Arrange the screen layout so that an Arrange page for each Project and the Tracks you wish to copy Regions to are visible. Drag the Regions from the source Project to the Destination Project (Figure 3.46).

Figure 3.45 (above)

Figure 3.46 (left)

The Finder Dock and what to do with it

OSX's Dock feature in the Finder is very useful for launching applications. But it can get in the way if you are using a program like Logic that requires a lot of screen real estate. There are several ways to improve the situation. These changes are made in the Dock section of OSX's System preferences application (Figure 3.47).

Figure 3.47

The Dock defaults to appear at the bottom of the screen. This can get in the way of using the window sliders. You may want to move it to the left or right side using the Position button (Figure 3.48).

Automatically hide and show the dock. Using this option makes the Dock disappear until you pass the mouse over it. Using the Magnification slider allows you to have a small dock – unless you move the mouse over a specific icon. Use the Dock Size slider to resize the dock.

You can remove the Dock completely using third-party programs. See Appendix 3 for web-links.

Play and Record Key Commands

While you can use the mouse to perform most record and play functions, you can speed up workflow by using some of the useful Key Commands relating to these functions.

Play

If you use any of the Key Commands for Play, you can use a Bluetooth keyboard (or one with a long lead) to Control Logic remotely. This is particularly useful if you are recording with a microphone and need to get as far away from the computer and monitor as possible. As you can see from the dot at the left of the list of Key Commands, many of these are available only as Key Commands (Figure 3.49).

Record

The same advantages apply here as for the Play Key Commands options. The computer keyboard can double as a remote record controller using these Key Commands (Figure 3.50).

Figure 3.48

Selection/Deselection Key Commands

All windows have various Key Commands that help with selection of Regions, notes or other objects.

Many of these only exist as key Commands and are quite specialized. They are particularly useful if you are performing repetitive tasks (see Figures 3.51 – 3.54).

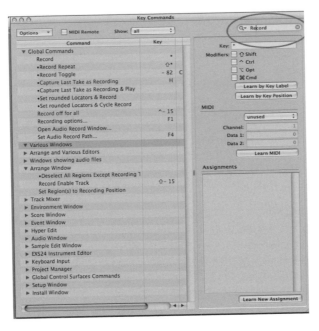

Figure 3.49

Figure 3.50

Figure 3.51

Figure 3.52

Figure 3.53

Figure 3.54

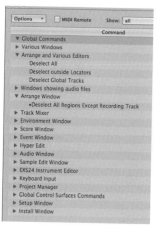

Parameter boxes in the Inspector

When you select a Region, Track, object or event in one of Logic's windows a Parameter box on the Inspector will detail the various parameters you can modify relating to that selection (Figure 3.55). You can usually change values by dragging the numbers up and down, double-clicking on the value and entering the value directly, or holding down on the little arrows to bring up a value selection menu (Figures 3.56, 3.57 and 3.58).

Figures 3.56 – 3.58 (left to right)

Figure 3.55

Figure 3.59

Tip

The Flex parameter allows audio to be affected by Logic Pro's Flex time feature. For more on this, see Chapter 4.

Tip

Logic Pro's audio files can be quantized just like MIDI files.

The small triangle on the Inspector opens or closes the box. This is useful if you are using Logic on a small screen (Figure 3.59 (right)).

You can show and hide the Parameter boxes using the Hide/Show Parameters Key Command.

Region Inspector

This displays the Parameters available from any selected Region or Regions. These parameters will be different depending on the Region type.

Figure 3.60
MIDI Region (Region on an Instrument or MIDI track.)

Figure 3.61
Audio Region.

Figure 3.62
Double-clicking on the name allows you to rename a Region or Regions.

Figure 3.64

- *Audio Regions: The Loop Parameter* will loop a Region until it meets another Region on the same Track. You can also loop Regions using by moving the mouse to the top right of the Region and dragging (Figure 3.64).
- *Audio Regions: The Fade Parameter* is active with audio Regions. You can choose a Fade type and value. You can also edit fades created by the Crossfade tool here (Figures 3.65 and 3.66).

Figure 3.65 and Figure 3.66 (right)

- *Audio Regions: The Curve Parameter* defines the slope of the crossfade. 0 is a linear type, increasing the value creates exponential curves (Figures 3.67 and 3.68).

Figure 3.67 and Figure 3.68

There is a default setting for crossfades in the general Audio preferences menu (Figure 3.69).

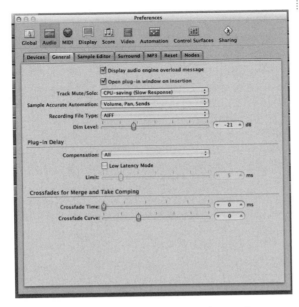

Figure 3.69

- *MIDI Regions: Dynamics Parameter.* This parameter can be used as a kind of MIDI compressor to 'squash' the dynamic range of a recording.
- *MIDI Regions: Gate Parameter.* The gate of a note refers to the time between pressing and releasing a key. The values which Logic use fall somewhere between staccato (short sharp notes) and legato (long notes). The 'Fix' value means extreme staccato, values below 100% shorten the note length, values above lengthen it. The 'Leg' value produces completely joined up playing.
- *MIDI Regions: Delay Parameter.* This parameter alters the time delay of selected Regions in ticks or milliseconds depending on the setting in the View menu. You can bring regions forwards or Backwards.

Track Inspector

The Parameters which appear here depends upon the type of Track selected. Clicking, and holding, on the icon itself opens a list where you can change the icon assigned to the instrument. Holding Shift as you do this leaves the menu open when you let go of the mouse key, so you can use the cursor keys to choose the icon.

Figure 3.70
Audio Track

Figure 3.71
Virtual Instrument
track

Figure 3.72
MIDI Track

Figure 3.74 (left)
Audio file playback. (including the
channel strip)
Figure 3.75
Virtual Instrument playback (including
the channel strip)

Info

Double clicking on the Instrument name opens a box where you can rename the Track.

Audio Track types and Parameters

Audio Track for playback of audio files, Virtual Instruments and inputs and outputs

The Instrument Track has extra Parameters – these are the same ones found on a MIDI track. As Virtual Instruments are played-back by MIDI, this makes complete sense.

Parameters

Core Audio This Parameter shows which of your CoreAudio drivers and outputs are being used on a Track. In Logic Pro 8 or later, you need to go into the Environment to change this value. Audio Tracks can be of the Track, Instrument, Input, Aux, Output Bus or Master type.

Figure 3.76

MIDI Track for the playback of external MIDI hardware devices

Figure 3.77

Double clicking on the Track name opens a box where you can rename the Track. Clicking to the right of this brings up a box containing the patch names of your MIDI device if you have entered these into a Multi-Instrument.

The small triangle on the Parameter box opens or closes the box. This is useful if you are using Logic on a small screen.

If the Parameter box is hidden or closed, holding down the Shift and Alt keys and clicking on the Track column will open the icon list.

Port. The pull-down menu here allows you to choose which physical MIDI output port your MIDI hardware is connected to.

Channel. This shows the MIDI channel of the selected instrument. It can be changed here with the mouse or by double clicking on the value.

Program. A tick in the box will transmit any changes made here to the MIDI device. The number on the right is the program change number. If you hold and click on this number, a pop up list appears from which you can select the program number. If you have assigned patch names to a Multi Instrument their names will appear here. Clicking to the left of this number will allow you to send bank select messages. You'll need to check your MIDI device handbook to see if your MIDI device uses bank select messages.

Volume. A tick in the box will transmit any changes to the MIDI device. MIDI volume controller data will be sent out if you change the number in the right hand column. .

Pan. This works in a similar way to the Vol parameter above.

Transpose. You can transpose all regions on a Track using this parameter.

Velocity. You can adjust the overall response to Velocity for all regions on a track.

Key Limiter. You can limit the range of notes played back by an instrument by setting a lower (left value) and higher (right value) note value here. All notes outside this range will not be played by the MIDI instrument.

Velocity limiter. You can limit the volume range of any instrument by setting a lower (left value) and higher (right value) value here. All notes whose velocity lies outside this range will not be played by the instrument.

No Transpose. If this is checked all Regions played by this instrument will be protected from transposition. Use this to keep drum sounds on their correct keys when transposing tracks.

No Reset. If this box is checked, no more reset messages will be sent to the instrument selected.

Style Auto. Clicking on this brings up the Score styles menu which are used in the Score editor. This is normally left set to Auto.

Tip

Don't forget to give your Tracks a useful icon. Click on the Icon and an icon list will appear.

Channel strip presets

If you click on the Setting box on an audio or Virtual instrument track, a pull down menu appears. These are Channel Strip presets – which are a series of

Figures 3.79 and 3.80

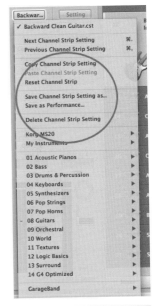

saved Channel Strip configurations. Audio, Bus, Aux and Instrument Tracks will load different presets (Figure 3.79). The Virtual Instrument Channel Strips include the Instruments themselves. Figure 3.80 shows 'Backwards clean guitar' selected.

- You can Save your own Channel Strip combinations or copy them and paste them into a New Channel Strip (Figure 3.81 (right)).
- You can also step backwards and forwards through Channel Strip presets using the menu items or the Key Commands. There are a series of Key Commands related to Channel strips.
- You can change Channel Strip presets using MIDI program change messages from an external MIDI controller. You must make sure these are sent on MIDI channel 1 though – messages sent on other channels will be sent to any plug-ins inserted on the Track and change their presets – assuming they respond to MIDI program changes.

Recording

Audio recording

Managing latency

Recording in Logic is affected by latency, that is, the time it takes for the audio to pass through the program, plug-ins and the audio input and output. If you are recording a vocalist, for example, what they hear when monitoring in the headphones after passing through Logic can be delayed causing a slight echo effect, which can be disconcerting for the singer. If you play Virtual Instruments, you may find that there is a delay between playing a note on a keyboard and the note actually sounding. There are a couple of ways to alleviate this problem.

You can work out the latency in milliseconds (ms) by the following equation.

$$latency (ms) = buffer size (samples) / recording sample frequency$$

Figure 4.1

So, for example, a buffer size of 256 and recording at 44.1kHz will give a latency of 5.8ms. Vocals and drums will usually need to be recorded with latencies under 6ms (256 buffer size). Guitarists can usually cope with latencies up to 12ms. They are used to the delay between amplifier or sound hole and ear (512 buffer size). Keyboards and Virtual instruments can often be played using latencies up to 20ms (1024 buffer size). Reduce the I/O buffer size in the Audio preferences window (Figure 4.1).

The lower the buffer size the lower the latency and thus the lower the delay to the vocalist will be. However, lowering the buffer size puts a greater strain on the CPU and will lower the number of plug-ins you can run. Go too low and you may also get CPU overloads.

Tip

Logic shows the 'round trip' Latency for each buffer size under the buffer setting pull down menu in the Audio Preferences window.

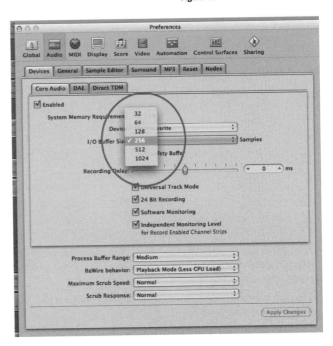

De-select software monitoring

When this is 'on', audio passes through Logic and any plug-ins inserted on the recording Track. You may have set up a plug-in reverb on this Track to help out a singer, for example. All this adds to the latency and the delay effects discussed above. Turning Software Monitoring to OFF will alleviate this problem – though you can't use any plug-ins on the recording Track.

- If you want to use Software Monitoring, use a plug-in which requires lower CPU power to run, such as the PlatinumVerb or Silververb, to minimize latency.
- Use an external mixer and reverb unit if you can't get the buffer settings low enough to please whoever you are recording. See below for more details.

Low latency mode

Tip

You can add a button to easily turn Low latency on and off by adding an icon to the Transport bar. Right click or CTRL click on the bar to add the icon (Figure 4.3).

If you're using Logic Pro 9, it has a low latency mode accessed from the General pane in the Audio preferences (Figure 4.2). When this is on, you can set a minimum acceptable latency for a session (5ms in this example). Logic achieves this by bypassing any plug-ins which are causing excess latency, so you may find that the sound changes if you're using a lot of plug-ins – especially if they are instanced on Auxes or Busses (Figure 4.3).

Use this feature when you want to add extra audio to a recording you've been mixing – it helps avoid any recordings being out of time with the previous audio. Don't forget to turn this off after you've done any extra recordings!

Figures 4.2 and 4.3

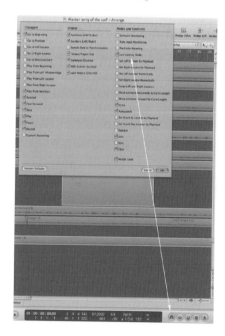

Safety i/o buffer

When working at low i/o buffer sizes you may experience drop-outs or crackling. Activating this may help reduce these, but as it will increase the latency of the system, it's better to us a larger buffer size.

Latency and external hardware – the i/o plug-in and Ping

Logic Pro's i/o plug-in allows you to route a signal out from a Channel strip to a piece of hardware such as a reverb or compressor and then back into the same Channel strip. It has a Ping button, which, when pressed, sends out a blip and calculates the round trip time in samples – this value is then used by the Automatic Delay Compensation (ADC) to bring this external hardware into time. For more on using external hardware with Logic Pro, see Chapter 9.

Figure 4.4

CPU (Central Processing Unit) overload problems

If you are finding that you're getting CoreAudio overload messages or that the CPU monitor is hitting the red, there are a couple of things you can do to help the problem. You can make the monitor visible by right or CTRL clicking on the Transport bar and adding it to the bar. You can get the old style CPU monitor by double clicking on the one in the Transport bar. There's also a Key Command available to toggle the CPU monitor on and off (Figure 4.4).

Freeze tracks

Freezing in Logic automatically mixes down the audio or Virtual Instrument data on a track to an audio file along with all plug-in effects. This 'combined' track is then automatically placed on the frozen Track. You can unfreeze a track at any time. Once frozen, the Track uses almost no CPU power – but you cannot edit any of the plug-ins on the Track unless you unfreeze it. You can, however edit volume and pan data. Freezing releases any CPU power used by any plug-ins on a track (Figure 4.5).

> **Tip**
>
> Make sure you can see the Freeze buttons on the Arrange page. They are displayed by right or CTRL clicking on the Track name or by selecting Configure track header.

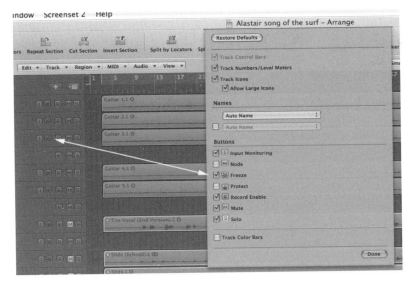

Figure 4.5

> **Tip**
>
> You can choose whether Freeze includes any plug-ins on a Track choose Source only from the pull down menu in the Track inspector. If you want to save CPU by freezing everything on a Track, choose Pre fader.

Increase buffer size

Increasing the buffer size to 512 or 1024 will relieve the load on the CPU, allowing you to use more plug-ins and Virtual instruments. You'll probably only do this after you've finished any recording due to the latency effects as described above.

Multiple processor CPU monitor and CoreAudio problems

On a multi-CPU processor Mac, the Logic System performance monitor has a meter for each processor. You may occasionally find that only one processor seems to be used and as that reaches maximum, Logic may complain with CoreAudio errors. If you start Logic playing, press stop and press start again, processing will usually be spread evenly across more processors.

Input/Output labels

You can label your inputs, outputs and busses, so you can select these by name from an Instrument, Audio or Buss object.

- Open the Mixer window
- Select the Options>I/O labels menu item.
- You can now name the inputs, outputs and busses (Figure 4.6).
- And then choose these in the Arrange page (Figure 4.7).

> **Info**
>
> On a multi processor system, you can force Logic to use the second processor to play back a Track that uses a lot of CPU power by selecting that Track on playback.

Figures 4.6 and 4.7

'Printing' effects onto a recording

Usually when you record, you only want to use an effect when you are monitoring, such as a reverb on vocals. Sometimes, however, you may want to record the effects along with the signal. An example of this is if you want to record a guitar through an amplifier simulator directly.

Normally, you'd record into Logic using an Audio Track object. However, if you do this, any plug-ins inserted onto that object will be heard when recording, but a clean signal will actually be recorded. Using the methods outlined below you can record the effects as well.

Printing the effects after recording

Right or CTRL clicking on the Region after recording and select Bounce in place, making sure that Destination is set to 'new track' and the Source to 'mute'. An advantage of working in this way is that the original, unprocessed, recording will be retained – so you can easily set up a simulated double track-

Figure 4.8

Figure 4.9

Figure 4.10

Figure 4.11

ing effect by copying this unprocessed Region to a new Track and setting a Delay value in the new Track's Inspector column. Panning this Track hard left and the 'printed' Region hard right creates a passable imitation of two different recordings with a widened stereo image.

Printing the effects while recording

Create an Audio Track and assign to it the inputs on your interface you want to use – the one the guitar is actually plugged into. Load in the effects you want to record. Click on the Input monitoring button (circled) so you can hear the effects and the input to the track (Figure 4.8). Assign the Track's output to a Bus (Figure 4.9).

Select another audio Track on the Arrange page – this will be the one used to do the actual recording. Assign the Bus described above as the input to the Track (Figure 4.10). Now when you record on this track, the audio from

Info

If you want to bring in external hardware to Logic see Chaper 9.

the track with all your effects will be routed here and to disk.

You can record arm both the track with the effects inserted and the second track which receives the input from the bus. This way, you can record both the 'dry' and effected sounds together.

Make sure the buffer size (set in the Audio Preferences window) is low enough for there to be no appreciable delay when you play the guitar. You should also set Plug-in delay compensation to 'Audio tracks and Instruments' or 'Off'; otherwise Logic will try to compensate for the delay in the playback chain.

Quantizing audio and beat slicing (strip silence)

You may be familiar with plug-ins and software that can take an audio file and slice it into chunks depending on various set parameters. These slices can them be moved around and quantized to create new parts. For example, you may have a 4 bar drum recording.

Figure 4.12

You may want to extract the snare and bass drum beats, move them around and change the timing, for example or quantize the beats to correct sloppy timing. You can also quantize audio using Flex mode – see later in this chapter for more information.

You need to make sure you have the Global Tracks feature visible Right or CTRL clicking on the Global Tracks area allows you to select the Beat mapping feature. Clicking on Detect will show the detected Transients on both the Region and the Global Track area. If Logic detects too many, or too few, transients use the + and – buttons to change the sensitivity of the detection until you have the tight amount of Transients. If you then right or CTRL click on the Region you can use the Slice at Transient Markers to split the Region into 'beats'.

Figure 4.13

If the Transients detected aren't quite 'on the beat', turn on Flex mode from the button on the Toolbar. Clicking on the Transients on the Region will add a small yellow arrow to the top of the Region. If you hold down the Alt key, you can finely drag the Transient markers to where you need them before slicing.

Figure 4.14

You can also use the Marquee tool's 'Snap to Transient' feature to split audio Regions 'on the beat' – see Chapter 3.

Transients can be edited directly in the Sample editor by clicking on the transedit icon (right). Then you can drag the white Transient markers around or delete them by double clicking on them.

Quantizing the Regions

If you've managed to put each drum beat into its own Region, you can then quantize the Regions. Here's how you do it. Highlight all the sliced Regions. Open the List editor – you'll see the Regions listed. If you hold down the Q

Figure 4.16

button you can choose the Quantize value and quantize the Regions (Figure 4.16).

Creating and manipulating 'takes' and 'mute and cycle' recording

A lot of Logic users work alone. It's often convenient to perform several 'takes' of a vocal or guitar solo, choose the best bits of the take and create a 'Comp' (Compilation) of the best bits. If you are doing this alone, you may also want to loop around the recording and record each take, muting the last. Here's how you do this in Logic.

Logic 9.x

Logic 8 and later introduced a new way to work with Takes. If you record on a Track and record over the same section again the old recording isn't delet- ed (if you have Replace turned off – see below). After subsequent recordings you'll see a little arrow appear on the left of the Region. You can set up a looping Cycle section if you want to work without stopping Logic – each pre- vious Take is automatically muted as the new one is recorded (Figure 4.17).

If you click on this it will reveal the Takes in the Takes folder (Figure 4.18 The top Region is the Compilation Region – this is the Region that you'll actually hear when you play back the Song and it consists of your chosen takes. Initially, the last recording is the one that plays back (the highlighted Region). But say we pre- ferred the first line from the second recording? If you click on the first recording the cursor changes. You can then click and drag the mouse

Figures 4.17 and 4.18

over the section you prefer. We'll call this the Take Region (Figure 4.19). You can see that this is reflected in the compilation Region (Figure 4.20). You can drag the ends of the selected Take and drag the whole selected Take using the mouse.

Figures 4.19 and 4.20

Figure 4.21

Take region

Now select the second phrase from the next Take. Continue until you have selected the Takes you require. If you click on on another Take Region above the selected Take Logic automatically sets that as the Take Region (Figures 4.21 and 4.22). Once you have selected your Take Regions (which will look something like Figure 4.23) you can close the Takes folder. Using the same arrow you used to open it. The Compilation Region now acts like a 'normal' Region and you can treat it like any other Logic Region.

Figure 4.22

Figure 4.23

Moving sections of Takes around

The Take folder has a small icon to the top right that toggles the Quick swipe comping mode on and off. When ON, parts of Takes can be selectively chosen as in the previous section. When OFF, you can drag a region around a selected section of a Take to highlight it (Figure 4.24). Move the mouse over

Figure 4.24

the Take until the + of the Marquee cursor appears, select the part of the Take required and then click on the Region to split it (Figure 4.25). This new Take Region can then be dragged around as if it was a 'normal' Region.

Figure 4.25

Why would you want to do this? You may, for example, want to use alternate takes as backing vocals or move an alternative Take that lies on the same timeline as the one you've already chosen to a position later in the Song. Or you may just want to correct small timing discrepancies in an otherwise perfect Take.

- You can use the Flex tool to change the timing of Takes in a Take folder. See later in the chapter for more information.
- You can use the 'old' method of Takes as described below by switching ON the Replace button on the Transport bar. Take folders are no longer created and each new Take is placed on top of the old one which is then Muted. After you've done all the passes you need, use the Arrange page Track>New for overlapped Regions command to drop each take onto separate Tracks. These can then be edited as detailed below.

Figure 4.25a

- You can automatically colour each take as you pass by ticking the box in the Recording settings section of the Project settings window (Figure 4.25a).

This makes it easy to see which of your takes contributes to the Comp (Figure 4.26). The 'starting' colour is chosen from the Color picker – which is opened from the Arrange page View menu.

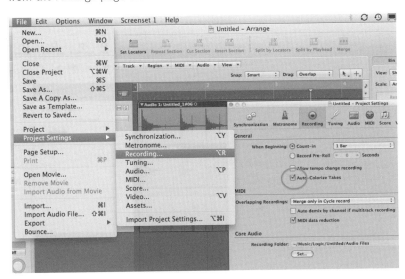

Figure 4.26

Creating and manipulating 'takes' and 'mute and cycle' recording without using Takes folders

It's often convenient to perform several takes of a vocal or guitar solo, choose the best bits of the take and create a 'Comp' (Compilation) of the best bits. If you are doing this alone, you may also want to loop around the recording and record each take, muting the last. Here's how you do this in Logic.

Looping around a section and recording

Figures 4.27 and 4.28

In the Song settings>Recording Preferences window, select 'Auto mute in cycle record' and 'Auto create in cycle record (Figure 4.27). Set a cycle Region that you want to loop around (Figure 4.28).

Start recording and play. As you reach the end of the looped Region, the SPL will move to the start of the loop again, a new recording begins and the previous recording will be muted. When you've finished your Takes press stop. Several Tracks and muted Regions ('Takes') will be created.

Selecting Takes

Once you have a series of Takes you'll want to choose the best bits and compile them onto one track – the 'Comp'. First, name each Take to 'Take 1', 'Take 2' and so on. De-Mute the Regions.

To keep easy track of each Take, it's a good idea to give them different colours. To do this, select a Take and select Colors from the View menu (left). A colour picker window opens.

- Choose a colour. Now select another Take and choose another colour. Repeat this until all Takes are coloured differently. Close the Color window. Use the scissors tool (or the Strip Silence as described earlier in the Chapter) to cut the Take into Regions. These might be a phrase from a Vocal or a Guitar Lick.

Figure 4.31

Figure 4.32

- Create a new Audio Track at the bottom of the Takes. Make sure all Tracks the Takes are on and Takes and this Track are the same (In this case It's Audio 2). Make sure the View menu Instrument name is checked and call the Track 'Comp' (Figure 4.33).
- Now audition each Region. Use the Solo and Mute buttons to listen to Regions individually. Drag any Regions you like to the lower 'Comp' Track. The Lowest tracks always mutes any of the same Tracks above so you'll only hear the 'Comp' Track. Pack any 'spare' takes into a folder in case you want to retrieve them later.

Figure 4.33

Figures 4.35 and 4.36

Drum editing using folders

If you are recording acoustic drums, it's likely that you'll have several tracks worth of recordings for bass drum, snare, hi-hats and so on. A typical drum recording could look like Figure 4.37. You may want to split these drum recordings into sections, such as 'verse', 'chorus', middle eight' and so on so you can move these around to experiment with different arrangements. In

Figure 4.37

Figure 4.38, Markers have been created showing the sections of the song. To create drum parts representing these sections, you could just split all the channels and drag these around.

But it's easy to get confused with so many tracks and you may find that you leave behind a recording when you copy and drag, or accidentally erase a recording altogether. It'd be much easier if you could just cut and paste a single track, which would affect all the drums together. We can do this in Logic using Folders. You can use several Folder-related Key Commands to navigate into and out of Folders (right).

First select all the drum recordings, then choose the Arrange page menu item Region>Folder>Pack folder

Figure 4.38

Figure 4.39

Figure 4.40

to create a Folder with all the drum recordings in it (Figure 4.40). If you double click on the Folder you can see all the drum recordings. To close the Folder click on the box at the top left of the window. Now you can cut and rename the folder as you please (Figure 4.42).

Figure 4..42

Tip

Use the text Tool and click on each Region to rename them or select and rename in the Region Parameter box.

Use the Goto next/Previous marker Key Commands to easily navigate Markers. Each section can then be dragged around to create new arrangements.

As drums are real instruments, cymbal crashes and other sustained sounds can overlap sections. You may have to go into a Folder and extend the shortened Regions to stop this happening (Figure 4.46), then extend the length of the Folder by dragging the length box (Figure 4.47). Double-click on a Folder to see its contents.

You can, of course, use this method for any instrument that has been recorded using multiple microphones, or, indeed, whole recordings.

Figure 4.46

Tip

You can return any recorded audio Regions to their original position using the Arrange Page > Audio > Move Regions to Original Record Position.

Figure 4.47

MIDI recording

Capture last take

As far as MIDI is concerned, Logic is always in record. So if Logic is playing, you can capture any MIDI recording (and this includes Virtual instruments) using the 'Capture last take' Key Command (Figure 4.48).

Tip

'Capture last take' doesn't work when recording audio. You need to press record first!

Figure 4.48

Tip

You can also place a Capture last Take icon on the Main Transport bar by adding it using the window which opens when you CTRL or right click on the Transport and open Configure Transport.

Advanced Quantization parameters

While the standard Region Inspector has most of the quantize parameters you'll need when editing Regions, there are times when finer control is required For this you can use the Advanced Quantization parameters accessible from the small pull down triangle.

Figure 4.49

The extra parameters are as follows:

Q-Strength – This determines how far a note is shifted towards the nearest quantize grid position. 100% is full quantization, 0% is no quantization.

Q-Range – All notes, whose distance from the nearest quantize grid position is the number of ticks set here, are not quantized. A value of 0 means every note is quantized. If you enter negative values (Far Quantize) only notes outside the selected Region are quantized. Use this to bring the worst played notes in a Region into time. If you enter positive values (Linear quantize) notes that are more 'laid back' that the rest of the Region are brought into line. This value is connected to the Q-strength setting

Q-Flam – Chords get spread out by this parameter. Positive values produce an upwards arpeggio, negative values a downward one. The first note is unaltered.

Q-Velocity –This parameter affects how much the velocity values of the Region are affected by velocity values in a Groove Template. At 0% the velocity is unaltered. At 100% it takes on the velocity values of the Groove template. Negative values make the deviation more extreme.

Q-Length – This is similar to Q-Velocity but affects the note lengths in the Region. 0% has no effect, ie the note lengths are unchanged. 100% means the note lengths become the same as the those in the template. negative values make the deviation more extreme.

MIDI (and Virtual instrument) multi-track recording

Multi player recording

You can record several MIDI tracks together all at the same time. If you have a keyboard player, MIDI guitar and drums, you can get a 'band' feel yet still have the luxury of editing notes and beats after the recording.

- Set the Project Settings>Recording preferences Auto demix by channel if multitrack recording.
- Connect your various MIDI devices to your MIDI interface. Make sure they are sending on different MIDI channels.
- Record enable the MIDI or Virtual instrument tracks you want to record on. In this example, two keyboards one transmitting on channel 1 the other on channel 2.Change the MIDI channel of the first Track to 1 and the second to 2.
- Record both instruments. One will be placed on the first Track, the other on the second.

Figure 4.51

Layer recording

You can also play two separate instruments together at the same time. Follow the instructions for multiple MIDI recording but de-delect the Settings>Recording preferences Auto demix by channel if multitrack recording.

Using Virtual instruments

Using Multi-timbral Virtual Instruments

Some Virtual instruments can respond to more than one MIDI channel at a time – just like old school hardware multi-timbral boxes. You might want MIDI channel 1 to control a bass sound, channel 2 a piano, channel 10 drums and so on. This is how you can do it in Logic.

Logic Pro 8 or later

Select the lowest Track on the Arrange page. Click on the '+' at the top of the Track list. The Create Tracks window opens. Select Software instrument, click the multi-timbral check box and type in the number of MIDI channels you'd like it to respond on – in this example eight.

Figure 4.52

- Clicking on Create will create 8 Tracks on the Arrange page, all set to the same Instrument. These will all have consecutive MIDI channels set (Figure 4.53).
- Now insert the multi-timbral instrument. In this case it's Garritan's Personal Orchestra (Figure 4.54).
- Selecting each of these Tracks will play back the sounds on the plug-in assigned to those MIDI channels.

Figure 4.53

Figure 4.54

Earlier versions of Logic

- Insert the multi-timbral virtual instrument in an Instrument object. In this case it's Instrument 1. Make sure each sound is set to receive on individual MIDI channels.

Figure 4.55

- Open the Environment and create a new page. Rename it something useful – in this case it's the Garritan Personal Orchestra (GPO), which can receive MIDI and play back different sounds on up to 8 MIDI channels (Figure 4.56 and 4.57).

Figures 4.56 and 4.57

- This instrument can respond on up to eight MIDI channels. Create a Multi Instrument object from the from the Environment page New menu (Figures 4.58 and 4.59).
- Rename the Multi Instrument to something useful (Figure 4.60).

Figures 4.58, 4.59 and 4.60

- Click on the box with a '1' in it. Make sure the box next to the Icon is ticked so the Instrument shows up in the Arrange page (Figure 4.61).

Now repeat this for the other seven channels (Figure 4.62).

Figure 4.61

- Hold down the Option key and click on the little arrow at the top right of the Multi Instrument and cable it to the GPO Virtual Instrument on Instrument 1. When Logic asks you if you want to change the Cable and Channel Port, choose 'remove' (Figures 4.63, 4.64,4.65).
- Now, each of these individual channels is available in the Arrange page. Selecting 'GPO channel 1' will play back the sound assigned to MIDI channel 1 on the GPO, 'GPO channel 1' will play MIDI channel 1 and so on (Figure 4.66).

Figure 4.62

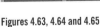

Figures 4.63, 4.64 and 4.65

Figure 4.66

You could also use single channel MIDI Instruments (Environment page>New menu). Create one; give it the required MIDI channel, rename it and cable it to the GPO Instrument (Hold down the Option Key and click on the arrow as above). Note the little stubby cable showing that the Instrument is cabled to another Layer in the Environment (Figure 4.67).

Figure 4.67

You then need to make six more Instruments. You can copy object by dragging them while holding down the Option key. Don't forget to change their MIDI channels. Note the little stubby cable showing that the Instrument is cabled to another Layer in the Environment (Figure 4.68).

Figure 4.68

These can then be chosen in the Arrange page in the same ways as for the Multi Instrument (Figure 4.69).

Using multi-timbral virtual instruments without multiple outputs

If you have a multi-timbral Virtual instrument that doesn't have separate outputs for each of its sounds, but you wish to process each sound assigned to each MIDI channel in a different way, use a different instance of the Virtual

Figure 4.69

Figure 4.70

instrument for each channel and load a different sound into each. In Figure 4.70, there are eight GPO instances each with different sounds loaded.

Multi output (multi channel) virtual instruments

Some virtual instruments Including Logic's own Ultrabeat and EXS24 can be used in their multiple output versions (Figure 4.71). What this means in practice is that you can send individual sounds from these instruments to Auxes and process these sounds further with plug-ins. Here's how you set this up using Ultrabeat as an example.

Figure 4.71

Logic 9

Instance a multi-output version of Ultrabeat on a Virtual instrument track.

Figure 4.72

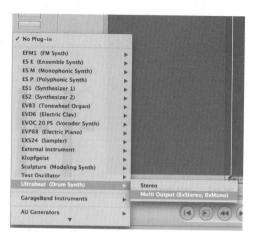

Open the Mixer tab. You'll see the Ultrabeat Instrument in the Mixer with a small '+' icon (Figure 4.73). Clicking on the '+" will create an Aux. Create as many Auxes as you need outputs. In this example, we'll send bass and snare drums through separate Auxes. So we'll create two and make them mono – click on the stereo icon on the Channel strip (Figure 4.74).

Figures 4.73 and 4.74

If you can't see any Auxes on the Mixer page make sure the Aux tab is enabled (Figure 4.75).

Figure 4.75

Figures 4.76 and 4.77

Figure 4.77

Now you need to route the output from Ultrabeat to these Auxes. If you click on the box under the I/O label you'll see a pull down menu where you can select the input to the Auxes. In this case, 17 and 18 (Figure 4.76).

- Now send the desired outputs from Ultrabeat to the Auxes – bass drum to 17, snare to 18 (Figure 4.77).
- Now you can add processing to the separate outputs and give them useful names (Figure 4.78).
- It helps to have these Auxes on the Arrange page in case you want to automate their levels.
- On the Arrange page, create as many new Audio Tracks as you have Auxes.
- Select each Track in turn and right or CTRL click on the Track name. Select the Track as an Aux from the pull down menu. You'll see the names you gave the Auxes in the mixer page (Figures 4.79 and 4.80).

Figure 4.78 (above) and Figure 4.79 (left)

Info

You can also use the Mixer page's Options > Create Arrange tracks for selected channel strips menu item.

Figure 4.80

Earlier versions of Logic

Instance the Multi channel version of Ultrabeat on an Instrument object – it's Instrument 4 in this example.

Figure 4.81

Open the Environment and create a new page – call it 'Ultrabeat multi out.'

Create a new Audio instrument from the New menu and double click on it to make it full size. Highlight it and select an Aux from the Channel pull down menu. Rename the object something like 'Ultrabeat output 1'. Make sure it's set to a mono channel (Figure 4.83).

Figures 4.83 – 4.85

If you click on the box next to 'I/O' on the object, you'll see a pull down menu appear. Choose 'Ultrabeat' 3 from the menu. Outputs 1 and 2 will always come out of the main Instrument object (Figure 4.84). Hold down the Option key and drag to copy the Audio object. Highlight the second object and select the next Aux from the Channel menu. It's important you do this before you perform the next actions (Figure 4.85). Rename the new Aux to 'Ultrabeat output 2' (Figure 4.86).

Figures 4.86 and 4.87 (right)

Click on the box next to 'I/O' on the object. Choose 'Ultrabeat' 4 from the   pull down menu (Figure 4.87).

Repeat until you have 14 objects, renaming then 'Ultrabeat 3', 'Ultrabeat 4' and so on. (Ultrabeat has 16 outputs – 2 on the Instrument channel the plug-in is inserted on and 14 here). Now you can add plug-in effects to each of these channels and adjust individual pan and volume settings.

General recording tips

Aliases of MIDI Regions

You can make aliases of MIDI Regions on the Arrange page. These are useful if you want to make sure that if you edit a Region any copies of that Region will also change. You create aliases of a MIDI Region by selecting it and using the MIDI>Alias>make menu item. You can turn an alias into a real copy (and therefore edit it separately from the original Region), from the same menu (Figure 4.90).

Figure 4.90

Looping Regions

You can loop any Region in two ways:

If you highlight the Region to be looped and click the Loop box on the Region parameter box, the Region will be looped until the end of the song or until another Region is encountered (Figure 4.91).

Figure 4.91

Info

Looping in this context isn't the same as using Apple Loops. More on these in Chapter 8.

If you drag the Region's top right corner the mouse pointer turns into a Looping tool. Dragging with this tool will loop the Region as far as you drag with the mouse. You can see you can choose where to end the loop.

Audio file formats

Logic can Import and bounce down to, several different file formats. Which of these you need to use depends on the project. Here are some tips on which format to use. The default file type is set in the General section of the Audio Preferences window (Figure 4.92).

Figure 4.92

AIFF

These are non-compressed files and are the 'standard' audio file used with the Macintosh – though they can be read on Windows machines too. It's usual for the default recording file type in Logic to be set to AIFF. AIFF files can be 16 or 24 bit and any sample rate up to Logic and your interface's maximum. When bounced, AIFF files can be read by most Mastering studios and the files are widely transferable across Macintosh audio software.

WAV

WAV files are the standard audio file type of the Windows PC. You may want to set the Logic default file type to WAV if you are exchanging data between your Mac and a Windows version of Logic. WAV files can be 16 or 24 bit and any sample rate up to Logic's maximum. When bouncing, you may want to use a WAV format if you want to master on a Windows machine or you are sending a mixdown to be used on a PC-based video editing program. Logic also supports Broadcast Wave files, which contain extra data such as time stamps for easy synchronisation.

MP3

This is a compressed audio format; that is, data is discarded to make the file size smaller. MP3 is the file type of choice if you want to e-mail your mixdowns or make your songs available for download on the Internet. MP3's can be bounced at varying qualities – the better the quality, the bigger the file.

AAC

This is Apple's own compressed format. It's similar in many ways to MP3, but arguably of better quality. Use this format for exporting into iTunes.

SDII

This is the full bandwidth file type of Digidesign's Pro Tools. SDII files can be 16 or 24 bit and any sample rate up to Logic's maximum You may want to use this as Logic's default file type if you will want to exchange Songs with Pro Tools users – though, these days, Pro Tools can also work with AIFF. Some Video editing houses, especially those working with Avid systems, use SDII files.

> **Tip**
>
> If you are sending files of mixdowns to be mastered or for use in a film or video, you need to make sure you send the format required by your customer. You may also want to use the ISO 9660 CD Burning format and send the files as data rather than Audio to maintain compatibility and quality.

CAF

Logic 8 introduced this new file format which overcomes the limited size of the above formats. CAF files can be greater than 4GB in size and give you about 13 hours recording time at 44.1kHz. WAV will only allow you to record for about 6 hours at this sample rate.

Sample rates

The Sample rate you can use for recording in Logic is defined by the capabilities of your Audio interface. The default recording rate is set either in your hardware's supplied software or the Audio MIDI setup application located in the Applications/Utilities folder, or from the Transport bar if you have this vis-

Figure 4.93

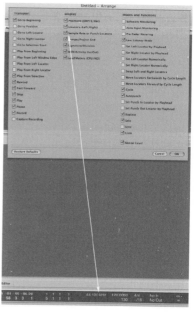

ible. If it's not, right or CTRL click on the bar to open the Preferences.

Higher sample rates yield higher recording quality. The highest frequency you can record is half that of the sample rate. So 44.1kHz can record up to 22.05kHz - just outside the human hearing range. 96kHz can record up to 48kHz. However there is a price to pay; higher sample rates require more hard disk space required to store the file. Also, if you plan finally to release your material on CD, that format is limited to 44.1kHz – and sample rate conversion is not without quality problems. Higher sampling rates do produce better quality recordings; though if you are recording electronic music you may not notice the difference. You'll also need higher quality ancillary equipment, especially monitoring, to hear the subtle improvements of the higher sample rates.

Figure 4.96 (far left)
Low sampling rate

Figure 4.97
High sampling rate

- Use a sample rate of 44.1kHz if you plan to release on audio CD.
- Use a sample rate of 48kHz if you are producing audio for DVD. This is the default DVD sampling rate for audio.
- Use a higher sample rate if you are recording acoustic sessions or want to release on a higher resolution format such as SACD.

Info

Logic performs automatic real-time sample rate conversion. If a project was recorded using a sample rate your Audio hardware does not support, it will be converted to one that it does support.

Bit level

The bit level used in recording is a defining factor of the audio quality of a recording. The lower the bit level used, the less well an analog signal will be reproduced, as the recording will use less steps to digitize the sound.

Figure 4.98 (far left)
16 bit resolution.

Figure 4.99
24 bit resolution.

CD is 16 bit and it describes 65535 discrete level values. A 4 bit recording system will only have 256. You can look at bit depth in the same way as resolution on a digital camera – the higher the bit depth the more 'in focus' the sound. In audio terms, the bit depth defines the dynamic range, measured in dB.

You can measure the dynamic range that will be given by a bit depth using the formula

6 x number of bits

So a 16 bit system has a dynamic range of 6 x 16 = 96dB, whereas a 4 bit system has a dynamic range of only 6 x 4 = 24dB

As you can see from the figures above, the greater the bit rate, the more discrete amplitude steps are described by the digitised waveform.

Info

A stereo sample recorded at 44.1kHz, 16 bit will take up approximately 10Mbof disk space per minute.

0dB

In analog recordings, it was common to push a recording level 'into the red' – i.e. over the 0dB meter mark. In an analog tape recorder, preamplifier, compressor or mixing desk, the distortion or saturation that occurs when you do this is pleasing to the ear. This is one of the reasons that some engineers swear by analog recording – the saturation is often used as an effect. In the digital domain things are very different. You should never record an input at a level over 0dB on your input meter, or have any playback channel or master output meter pass this limit. The distortion in digital systems when you do this isn't pleasant; unless you're actually trying to make unpleasant noises that is!

Monitoring

When you record into Logic there are a few requirements everyone will need.

- To be able to hear what you are recording
- To be able to hear what has previously been recorded
- To be able to monitor effects – but not necessarily record them
- To be able to replace sections that were badly played or sung.

In all these situations you'll need to hear or 'monitor' what you are doing. There are several ways to do this in Logic.

Software monitoring

This is turned on from Logic's Audio Preferences>Audio>Devices window.

Figure 4.101

When this is set to 'ON' the audio path through Logic is as detailed in Figure 4.102. As you can see, the audio passing through Logic is subject to the latency in the system, as it takes time to pass through all the stages, so you may want to check out the section covering latency earlier in this chapter. The advantage of software monitoring is that you can apply monitoring-only effects to the recording channel. For example, its nice for a vocalist to hear a bit of reverb while singing, but record the vocals dry.

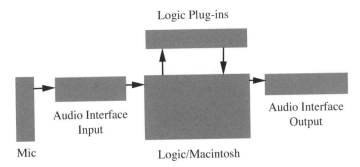

Logic Plug-ins

Audio Interface Input

Logic/Macintosh

Audio Interface Output

Mic

Figure 4.102

Hardware monitoring

If you turn software monitoring to 'off' you wont have any latency problems, but you won't be able to add a software reverb plug-in to the recording Audio object. You can get around this by using a mixer and an external reverb.

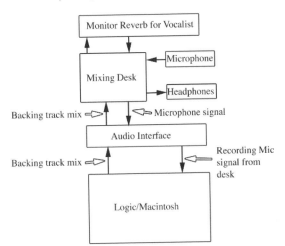

Monitor Reverb for Vocalist

Microphone

Mixing Desk

Headphones

Backing track mix ⇨   ⇦ Microphone signal

Audio Interface

Backing track mix ⇨   Recording Mic signal from desk ⇦

Logic/Macintosh

Figure 4.103

Info

Some Audio interfaces have a direct monitoring feature that sends the audio from the input directly to the output thus eliminating latency. The same caveats as for Software monitoring being set to OFF apply to these as well.

Punching in

In the old tape-based recording days, where tracks were limited, an engineer would often replace mistakes by 'punching-in'. This entailed rewinding the tape to a position before the mistake, pressing play and then record *exactly at the right point*. Even a slight error could mean that good material before and after the punch-in could be lost. You can emulate this technique in Logic using the locators and the punch-in button on the Transport bar, but as we now effectively have an unlimited amount of tracks, there's a much easier way to perform the same operation.

First locate the section of the recording that you want to replace (Figure 4.104). Use the Scissors tool, Marquee tool or the 'Split Regions/Events by Song Position' Key Command. Delete the offending Region (Figure 4.105).

Figures 4.104 and 4.105

Figures 4.106 and 4.107

Create another Audio Track under the old recording. Select the Track (Figure 4.106). Record the new material onto this new Track. You'll be able to hear the old recording up to the error (Figure 4.107). Drag the ends of the new recording so they line up with the gaps on the original recording Track, and drag the Region into the gap.

Apply crossfades if needed. You may also need to fine-tune the ends of each Region.

Crossfades

When you cut up audio files and butt discontinuous Regions up against each other, you'll often get a click or a level change as the play head plays over the join. To cure this problem, you'll need to use crossfades.

 Select the crossfade tool from the Toolbox. Drag it over the join. You'll see the fade being drawn. You can change the slope and type of the fade in the Parameter box. You may only need very small values to clear up a click. Too high a value may sound like a fade out.

Curved crossfades often sound more natural than a simple 'X' shape fade (Figure 4.113). If there is a discontinuity between the Regions, use Volume Automation to adjust the levels (Figure 4.114).

The default crossfade values are found in the General section, Audio Preferences window.

Figure 4.113

Figure 4.114

Tempo tips

Most recording people do these days is done to a strict tempo. However, if you are recording 'real' musicians, or you've recorded something with spur of the moment inspiration, you may still want to perform quantizing or tempo editing on the data. For this you'll need to get Logic to understand the tempo of your recording.

Using the computer keyboard to set the tempo

Say, for example you have pre-recorded music on tape and you want to set the tempo of Logic Pro to the same tempo. You can use a computer keyboard key to enter this tempo.

Using the tempo interpreter

Assign the Key Command Tap tempo in the Key Commands window (right) to a suitable computer key. Open the Tempo interpreter from the Options>Tempo menu.

You can set the following parameter values:

Tap step – sets the note value that the taps will be describing. Best results will be obtained by using larger values. Try 1/4 note to start.
Window (Ticks) – sets a window within which incoming taps are used. Taps outside this window are ignored. The narrower the window you can use, the better.
Tempo response – this adjusts the sensitivity to tempo changes. The larger the values the greater the sensitivity. Start with 4.
Max Tempo change – sets the maximum tempo change possible. Select as small a value as possible to reduce the tempo fluctuations to a minimum.
Tap Count-in – Logic starts responding to incoming taps after this count-in period has passed.
Smoothing – when on, smoothes out large changes in the incoming tempo.
Tempo recording - when on, a tempo list is created as you tap.
Pre – displays all the incoming taps
Post – displays only taps that fall in the above set parameters

Close the tap tempo windows. Now start tapping on the key you set up in the Key Command window. After the count-in, Logic Pro will start at the tempo of the tapping. The tempo determined is displayed in the Transport bar.

Beat mapping and the Global Track

This allows you to set the tempo of a song after recording, allowing you to play freely and worry about the tempo afterwards. Once you have 'beat mapped' the recording, you'll get all the advantages of recording with a metronome, such as;

- The metronome click will be in time
- You can quantize Regions
- MIDI and Apple loops will automatically adjust to the tempo of the song.
- It helps with interpretation in the Score editor.

When using beat mapping you connect the beats present in your recording to the bar positions on the Beat mapping Track window. Here are a couple of examples.

Select the beat mapping Global Track from the Arrange Page View>Configure Global Tracks menu. Make sure the Global Track is visible from the same View menu.

MIDI or Virtual instrument Regions

Record a Region without using the Metronome. Note that the initial tempo set in Logic is 120 bpm (beats per minute). If you open the Matrix editor, you can see where the beats actually lie in the performance. Note that Logic shows the notes as small coloured lines.

Figure 4.119

The next part can be performed in either the Matrix editor or Arrange page (or Hyper editor, for that matter).

* Select the first note in the Region.
* Click and hold on the first beat in the Beat mapping track.
* You'll see that the line will turn yellow and that 'Set Beat' will appear in a small window.
* Drag the mouse (while still holding down the mouse key) to the first note in the Region or to the first note in the beat mapping Track.

Figure 4.120

Figure 4.121
Before dragging.

Figure 4.122
Yellow line.

Figure 4.123
After dragging.

- Release the mouse key. You'll see that the first note in the Region is aligned to the first note of the bar in the Beat mapping track.
- Now select the note that you consider to be the first in the next bar.
- Click and drag the yellow line from the bar line to the note in the same way as for the first bar.
- Release the mouse key. You'll see that the second note selected in the Region is aligned to the second bar of Beat mapping track.

- Repeat for all the bars in the Region (this Region has 4 bars of playing).

- Now repeat for any notes within the bar if needed.

Logic will create tempo changes for each bar – you can see these if you open the Tempo Global Track (Figure 4.127). If you just set the tempo for the first bar or a Region, you can then quantize the entire Region using this tempo value as a guide. To delete set tempo points, just click using the erase tool.

Figure 4.127

Audio Regions
To map an audio Region. Logic must determine rhythmically significant spots in the recording. For a drum snippet, this could be the bass drum or hi-hat part. These spots are usually louder or more prominent and Logic can use this to analyse the recording.

- Select an audio Region. This is a 4 bar drum loop. You'll see that Logic shows the transients in the Beat mapping Global Track.
- Click on Analyze to detect the transients in the Audio file.

You'll see that Logic has detected too many transients. There are a couple of parameters you may like to consider when trying to use Beat mapping with audio Regions.

Transient detection sensitivity.
A high Transient detection sensitivity will detect more transients and give you more points in which to use for Beat Mapping. This may or may not be a good thing, depending on the audio Region – you may detect transients that are not really there. As this works in real time, you can click on the + and – buttons to see the effect of changing the sensitivity.

Once you have detected the transients, you can Beat map the tempo in exactly the same way as for MIDI Regions.

If you record a MIDI Region (using an external sound source or Virtual instrument) with a Metronome, you can use the Beats from Region button to 'map' the tempo from this MIDI Region to the song.

Record a Region with a fixed tempo close to the one of the audio file. Edit the beats in the Region until they sync with the audio file beats. Then click the Beats from Region button. Logic will create tempo changes to preserve the timing.

Lock SMPTE position

If you're working to picture, there'll probably be times you'll want to make sure some Regions are locked into position even if you change the Tempo. You can make sure they stay put whatever you do to the Temp from the Region>Lock/Unlock Tempo Position menu items. It's handy to set these up as Key Commands too.

Track protection

You can prevent the accidental change or deletion of a Track by using the Track protect buttons. These can be made visible on the Arrange page from the View>Track protect buttons menu item.

Flex time – working with Audio in Logic

Audio is a much more fluid entity in Logic Pro 9 in comparison to earlier versions. Logic's Flex mode allows you to stretch and warp audio either directly, using the Flex tool or by manipulating Flex markers.

The Flex tool

If you select this tool and drag it across an audio file, you'll see that the waveform stretches along with the tool, elongating the audio while keeping the pitch the same. If Flex mode hasn't been enabled, Logic will ask you to turn it on and select a Flex mode suitable for the audio you are trying to edit.

Figure 4.128

The different modes have useful help tips in the window to assist you in choosing the correct mode. Slicing creates Transient markers in the Beat mapping Global Track so you can slice the Region into sections defined by the Transients.

Tip

Make the Arrange page waveforms larger by clicking and using the slider on the Waveform display size icon.

Figure 4.130

Holding down the Alt key while dragging a Flex marker just moves its position without changing the audio.

Clicking on the Flex icon on the Toolbar, switches the Flex mode display on – you'll see that a simple swipe has created three Transient or Flex markers. You can drag these markers around to finely edit the audio Region (Figure 4.130).

If you use the Marquee tool to highlight a part of the Region, then use the Arrow tool to drag this area, 4 flex markers are created. This makes it easy to drag an uncompressed area within an area that is compressed or expanded. This is useful for placing a section within a Region by compressing or expanding audio before and after the Marquee selection. This may be a better option than cutting and dragging in some cases (Figure 4.131).

When in Flex mode, you can create Flex markers by clicking on the upper half of the waveform. The Pointer turns into a flex marker tool.

Figure 4.131

- If you click on the bottom half of the waveform, three Flex markers will be created.
- If you create a Marquee selection before you create Flex markers, the bounds of the selection will define where the Flex markers are created.
- You can easily add Flex markers anywhere in a Region allowing you to move specific portions of audio at will.

Time compression and expansion

When you drag a Flex marker, you'll notice that the colour of the Region changes depending on what's happening.

Green – signifies time compression. The greener the Region, the more compressed.
Orange – signifies time expansion. The more orange the Region, the more expanded it is.
Red – signifies high compression – which may or may not produce useable effects!

Flex markers can be deleted by double clicking on them. Holding down the Alt/Option key while dragging at the bottom of the start and end of a Region will compress or expand a whole Region.

Using Flex time with Beat Matching

If you've created some Transient markers using the Beat Mapping on a drum part, for example, you can match Flex markers on another Track, such as a guitar part, to correct timing errors. If you drag a Flex marker to one of the

Figure 4.132

faint blue lines (the Transient markers) it will snap to the position of the Transient marker (Figure 4.132).

The Flex modes

When Flex mode is on, the different Flex modes can be selected from the Pull down menu on a Track (Figure 4.133).

Figure 4.133

Each mode has specific Parameters displayed in the Region Inspector (Figure 4.134).

Figure 4.134

Slicing – a another way to cut audio when using percussive material

Earlier in the chapter we used Beat matching to slice audio at Transient markers in a Region. Using the Slicing Flex mode can achieve similar results. Make sure the Track list pull down menu is set to OFF then turn Flex mode off too.

Figure 4.135

Select the Flex tool and click on the Region. Choose Slicing from the pull down menu which appears (Figure 4.135). Now turn Flex mode on. You'll see the created Transients in the Region (Figure 4.136).

Figure 4.136

The Parameters available for Slicing mode are:

Fill Gaps – this extends the release phase of slices in passages up to the next slic to close any audible gaps.
Decay – this sets a time in seconds for the decay of each slice – again, adjusting this setting can help between transitions on slices..
Slice Length – this shortens each slice by a percentage value.

Rhythmic
The Rhythmic flex mode is most suitable for non-monophonic pitched material. These could be guitars, keyboards or indeed, Apple Loops. The Parameters available for Rhythmic mode are:

Loop Length – Logic creates a looped section at the end of a time-expanded slice. This sets the length of the loop.
Decay – defines a decay value for the looped area.
Loop Offset – allows you to move the looped area up to 100 ms to the left. This is useful for removing transients that may bleed into the lopped area.

Like a lot of parameters in Logic, these are best set by ear, as the audio being processed will have a large effect on the way they interact.

Monophonic

The Monophonic flex mode is good for solo vocals and monophonic solo instruments – melody and bass lines, for example. For best time-stretching quality, record dry without any effects.

Percussive – this setting makes sure Logic preserves the timing for all kinds of percussive monophonic tonal material such as bass and plucked instruments. Unselect it if you're processing instruments such as strings, flutes or other non percussive instruments.

Polyphonic

Use this mode on complex material such as guitar or keyboard chords or even whole mixes. The parameters available in polyphonic mode are:

Complex – this allows for the preservation of transients when switched on – but may cause glitches, so it's best to experiment.

Tempophone – intended as a special effects generator – a kind of granular synthesizer which breaks the audop up and plays it back in various ways defined by the parameters below.

Grain Size – this produces artifacts similar to ring modulation, where grain size determines the modulation frequency. It has a range of 0.10 to 500.00. Useful for clanging distorted sounds.

Crossfade – a value of zero produces the full effect. Increasing it to 1 makes the sound softer

Speed

This is the classic time stretching effect in that it affects both tempo and pitch.

Speeding up and slowing down

A popular old trick used with tape machines was performed by changing the speed of the motor to change the pitch and duration of a recording – the varispeed effect. Logic Pro 9 can simulate this – but note that it affects all of a Project. You turn the Varispeed on from the Transport bar button – if it's not there add it using the Customize option by CTRL or right clicking on the bar.

Figure 4.137

Once on, Clicking on the Varispeed Transport bar area reveals a menu.

Figure 4.137

By its nature, Tape varispeed affected both tempo and pitch. In Logic, we can select both or just speed and, if we want, MIDI (and Virtual Instruments) to be affected too. A specific tempo or pitch can be defined as well.

To use this technique on single audio Regions, use the Export as audio file menu (by CTRL or right clicking on Regions) to export individual Regions for re-importing.

Slowing everything down

You can create a gradual slow down of speed of a Region, such as that created when you turn off a turntable, by creating a Fade and selecting the Speed up or Slow down parameters in the Inspector (which depends on if the fade is at the start of the Region or at the end.) (Figure 4.139).

Figure 4.139

Drum Replacement

Even if you manage to record a beautifully tuned, well played drum kit in a lovely sounding room, you may still find that some of the individual sounds in the kit don't stand up on their own – or against other commercially released tracks. Recording a kit is a compromise; microphones interact, players are inconsistent. A common 'trick' is to replace or enhance one or more of the elements of a recorded kit with a sample, for example the bass or snare drums. While Logic provides many pre-recorded samples, you can use your own – for example, you could add pristine bass and snare samples using the same drummer, kits and recording set up as for the track. You get the best of both worlds – a real, dynamic performance with the 'oomph' a well-recorded sample can add.

First select a Track containing drum parts – in this case, it's a bass drum. Then choose The Drum Replacement/Doubling item from the Arrange page Track menu. The drum replacement menu opens (Figure 4.140). You'll see that Logic has helpfully opened the Media browser and listed all available instruments which relate to the instrument type selected (Figure 4.141).

You can use any of Logic's Instruments on the automatically created Software Instrument/MIDI Track under the processed Audio Track – or indeed, any AU plug-in or external MIDI hardware.

Logic analyses the transients in the Regions on the Track and places yellow lines at these positions. The Relative Threshold slider lets you decide what exactly is a Threshold – it works in real time. There's also a Prelisten button which plays back both original and new sample to help you check for missed notes or phasing problems. If you find trhat you're getting a 'flam' effect, try changing the Timing offset to compensate. The Set average attack time but-

Figure 4.140

ton can automatically set this offset to attempt to accurately align the start of Transients.

Tip

If you are finding that other drums in a recording, for example snare bleed into a bass drum track, add a noise gate to the bass drum, set it so that only the bass drum is heard, right or CTRL click on the Region and use the Bounce in place to create a new Audio file on a new Track – then use this Track to do your drum replacement. Remember to leave the Bypass plug-ins unchecked – it may also help to normalize the bounce.

Bounce Regions In Place

Name: Bass Drum_bip_1_bip

Destination: ● New Track
○ Selected Track

Source: ○ Leave
● Mute
○ Delete

☐ Include Instrument Multi-Outputs

☐ Bypass Effect Plug-ins

☑ Include Audio Tail in File
☐ Include Audio Tail in Region

☐ Include Volume/Pan Automation

Normalize: Off

Restore Defaults   Cancel   OK

You can choose whether to mix the original in with the doubled sample (Doubling) or replace it entirely (Replacement).

The Trigger note allows you to set what note is generated in the new MIDI Regions. For example, bass drums are usually on a C1 note (MIDI note number 31). However, if you're using custom samples you may want to change this – though you can, of course, change this by editing the data directly in the MIDI Regions. Clicking on OK closes the window leaving the original audio muted if you chose Replacement.

Easy creation of EXS24 sampler Instruments

You can convert one of your bass drum Regions into samples to be used with the drum replacement feature, by selecting the Region, right or CTRL clicking on it and selecting Convert to new Sampler Track. A new Window opens (Figure 4.143).

If you select Transient Markers, an EXS instrument is created with each detected bass drum placed on different keys. These can then be used during drum replacement as described above,

You can use any Region to create EXS24 Instruments. These can then be played like regular instruments and easily transposed and processed.

Figure 4.143

Quantizing audio the easy way using Flex mode

Though you can slice audio regions and use the standard quantize features in the Inspector, an easier way to bring your audio into time is to use the standard quantize feature directly. Switch Flex mode on, choose a Flex type from the pull down menu and select the quantize value from the Inspector. In Figure 4.144, a drum loop has been copied and quantized to 1/8th note. This is almost exactly the same way as you treat MIDI data.

Figure 4.144

Plug-ins

Logic and Audio Units

Logic uses the Audio Unit (AU) standard for plug-ins introduced by Apple with OSX. AU plug-ins are located in the Library/Audio/Plug-ins/Components folder and are loaded when Logic boots. You might want to check out Logic's AU manager in Chapter 1 as AU plug-in verification problems are a common cause of instability problems.

Apple's Audio Unit plug-ins

Apple ship several useful plug-ins, which can be found in the Audio Unit pull down menu – so they are often missed. Don't ignore these though. They may look pretty simple but some of them are extremely useful.

Figure 5.1
Apple's AU plug-ins.

AUMatrixReverb is a fine sounding reverb unit. It's probably an improvement on Logic's Platinumverb, although the Space Designer outclasses it – but then again, it uses a lot less CPU resources.

Figure 5.2
AUMatrixReverb

AUPitch uses OSX 10.4.x's pitch changing algorithms to smoothly change the pitch of audio files. It produces a much better result than the Sample editor's Time Machine. The algorithms are also available in the Arrange page when using the 'fit to the bar' feature. See Chapter 7 for more on this.

Figure 5.3
AUPitch

AUNetSend and AUNetReceive

These two operate as a pair. You can use AUNetSend to send audio over a network and receive the Audio on another Mac running AUNetReceive. Here's how you do it:

Load AUNetSend on the first Mac. In this example, it's instanced on a Piano sound in Logic. If you then load AUNetReceive on the second Mac, it will pick up the AUNetSend on the first Mac – assuming they are both networked together (Figures 5.5 and 5.6).

Figure 5.4

Figure 5.5

Figure 5.6

Playing the piano plug-in on the first Mac will sound through the second Mac. You can send any audio this way, at a variety of quality levels.

Figure 5.7

Tip

If you find that you can't connect AUNetSend to AUNetReceive try switching off the Firewall in the System Preferences Sharing window.

Garageband instruments

Logic comes with the full range of Virtual instruments that is also supplied with Garageband – ostensibly for Garageband compatibility. These are simplified versions of Logic's own plug-ins, but again, don't ignore them. They are just as fine sounding and their simplified interfaces lend themselves to rapid experimentation.

Figure 5.9

Info

You can only wrap VST plug-ins that have been converted for use under OSX with Logic. You cannot use OS9 or Windows VST plug-ins.

Using VST plug-ins in Logic

Although Logic itself cannot use VST plug-ins directly, It's AU only, you can circumvent this limitation with some third-party software. These so-called VST 'wrappers' create a shell that fools Logic into believing it is loading an AU plug-in.

Third-party plug-ins in Logic

While Logic has a plug-in to suit most occasions, there will always be times when you want to use a particular synthesizer, compressor or EQ. Logic supports third-party AU plug-ins. Usually these are installed automatically when you run the plug-in installer program, but occasionally you have to install them yourself.

AU plug-ins are stored in the Library/Audio/Plug-ins/Components folder. If your third-party AU plug-in doesn't appear in the Channel striplist, make sure it's not been disabled by Logic's AU manager. See Chapter 1 for more on this.

Effects plug-ins

Logic has several plug-ins that aren't immediately obvious in their functions

BPM Counter

This can detect the tempo of a recording when inserted on the Track it is playing on. It's useful if you have some drum loops and you don't know the tempo, for example.

Correlation meter

This meter helps you to check if your recordings will be mono-compatible – very useful for TV and radio work. If the meter is reading positive, the more mono compatible your recording is. If it's negative, there will be phase cancellations when the Song is played in mono.

Direction mixer

This is a sophisticated Pan controller that can also deal with MS (Middle and Side) encoded audio. As you turn the DirMixer direction control to the right the signal will pan towards the right – it's hard right at 90 degrees. As you continue turning the control clockwise, the signal will appear to swap channels – almost as if the signal is being panned around in a circle. The Basis control sets the width of this spread. A value of 0 gives a mono signal. When the value is greater than 1, the signal appears to come from outside the speakers, which is useful for ambient effects.

Gain

This plug-in allows you to increase the gain of any signal, along with left/right balance. It's useful if you have something recorded at a really low level or a plug-in instrument that has a low output level. You could also use it to match levels between plug-ins instanced on the same Track.

If you insert a Gain plug-in on the Master output track, you can use it to check out playback in mono.

You can invert the phase of the left and/or right channel signal to create a wide special effect. It's also useful when you have Tracks recorded with microphones that have phase problems.

I/O

This plug-in allows you to route audio into and out of Logic via the physical inputs and outputs of your Audio interface. You choose the required channel from the Input and Output pull down menus – how many are there depends on your interface. You can adjust the input and output levels. Use this plug-in to send and return to a hardware effects unit (such as a reverb) so it can be used in-line with plug-in effects. For more on this see Chapter 4.

Level meter

This is a high-resolution level meter. Insert this on the Master output to get a better picture of your levels. You can choose from 3 different modes for the meter. Peak shows the maximum level with a hold function so you can see what's going on over a whole song. RMS shows the average level. Peak & RMS combines the two modes.

Multimeter

In Analyser mode, this plug-in shows a real-time graphic display of the frequency range of a signal. You can use it on whole mixes to see what the spectral balance of your mix is like and compare it with commercial releases.

In Goniometer mode, the plug-in helps you see any phase problems in a stereo signal. If you get signal cancellations along the M line, you have phase problems – something is canceling out in the centre signal. The multimeter also has a Correlation meter (see above)

Test Oscillator

Mainly designed to help produce impulse responses for Space Designer, you can also use it as a sine wave effects generator. Try using it as a side chain input to the Ring Modulator plug-in.

Tuner

This is a handy chromatic tuner. Insert it onto a recording Track and use it to tune a guitar.

Enhanced Timer

This plug-in allows you to quantize audio in a similar fashion to MIDI data. It's a simple plug-in. Choose the grid you want to quantize to and adjust the slider until you get the desired effect.

Figure 5.21
The Enhanced Timer plug-in only works if it's inserted in the *first* slot on a channel.

Pitch Correction

This plug-in attempts to bring out of tune audio back into tune in real-time (Figure 5.22). This plug-in can help with correcting minor deviations from pitch (shown on the 'keyboard' display). The faster the response setting, the more likely you'll hear artifacts. These can be used creatively as many a hit record will testify!

• Choose the range of the signal to be corrected. Low for bass sounds, such as Fretless Bass. Choose Normal for those with high frequency content, such as vocals.
• Choose a scale and root note if you can.
• You can bypass certain notes from the correction process.

Figure 5.22
The Pitch Correction plug-in.

Info

You can use the Apple AUPitch plug-in to process individual notes that are out of tune. Isolate the offending note and split it from the surrounding region using the Marquee tool.

You can automate the pitch correction plug-in parameters to get the right settings for different parts of a song.

Figure 5.23

Drag it to another Track. Convert it to an independent audio file using the Arrange page>Audio>Convert Regions to New audio files. Insert the AUPitch plug-in on the Track.

Figure 5.24

Adjust the offending Region. You may want to loop around a wider section of the Song to hear it in context. Select the Region and export it using the File>Export>Export Region as Audio file. Make sure the 'Add resulting files to Audio Window is set.

Figure 5.25

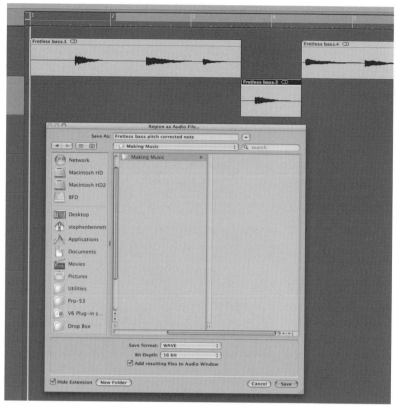

Open the Audio window; drag the processed Region to the gap in the original Track and mute the processed Region.

Figure 5.28

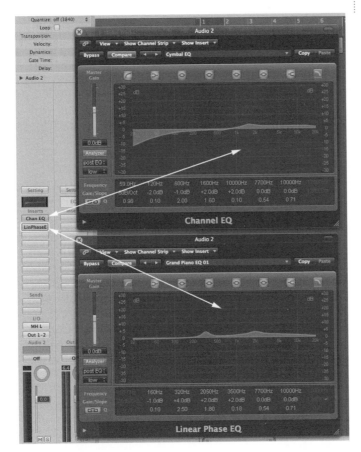

Channel EQ and Linear Phase EQ

At first glance, these two EQ's may look very similar and, in fact, you can copy presets between them. However, sonically, they are quite different.

The difference is indicated in the name. The Linear Phase EQ preserves the phase of the EQ at all settings. In a normal EQ (such as the Channel EQ) phase changes as you change the settings. This isn't always a problem as these phase changes are part of the reason some EQs sound 'nicer' than others. The Linear Phase EQ could be said to sound 'neutral' whatever the setting – even at extreme EQ settings, it doesn't impart it's own character. The downside of the Linear Phase EQ is that it uses more CPU power than the humble Channel EQ.

- Use the Channel EQ for general EQ duties or when you want to impart its sound on a Track.
- Use the Linear Phase EQ when you want to EQ without changing the overall nature of the sound. This is particularly useful when mastering a mix.

Info

The Linear Phase EQ and Channel EQ have an Analyzer button. When this is ON, a plot is displayed of the frequency spectrum of any audio passing through the EQ. You can choose the resolution of this plot – how smooth it is. The higher the resolution the slower the frequency plot will be updated. The Pre EQ/Post EQ toggle allows you to see the effect on the spectrum of the EQ. You can use this analyzer to compare the spectrum of a commercial CD and compare it to your mixes

Match EQ

The Match EQ takes this comparison a stage further by actually allowing you to impose the frequency spectrum of an audio recording onto another. The idea is that you can take a recording you like the sound of and modify yours to suit using the Match EQ. Bear in mind that the Match EQ can't perform

Figure 5.30

miracles – there's more to a sound than just EQ. However, You may want to try the following:

- Impose the EQ curve of a commercial song you like on one of your own.
- Impose the EQ curve of acoustic guitar recorded with a microphone onto one recorded with a pickup – or even an electric guitar.
- Impose the EQ curve of a sitar on a guitar – or two completely different instruments for an unusual effect.

Here's how to use the match EQ. Instance the match EQ on a Track. The Region on the Track is the one we are trying to impose the EQ onto. Hold down the Control key and click (or right click) on the Template Learn box.

Figure 5.31

Load in the source file – the audio file you want to use as your template EQ. This could be a commercial CD whose frequency spectrum you want to emulate. You'll see the spectrum of this file displayed.

Figure 5.32

Click on the Current Material Match button. The EQ spectrum is imposed

Figure 5.33

onto the Track which the match EQ is inserted on. You can use the Apply slider to change the intensity of the EQ change.

MultiPressor and the AUMultiband Compressor

These are both plug-ins that split the audio into several separate audio bands and each is then compressed separately. With a normal compressor, if you try to compress a signal with a prominent bass, say, that will have a disproportionate effect on the compression effect. This is particularly a problem when compressing whole mixes. So the idea with a Mult-band compressor is to split the signal into bass, mids and high frequencies and compress these separately thus minimizing these problems. They are particularly useful when mastering a stereo mix.

The AUMultiband Compressor

This is a simple (though nice sounding) multi-band compressor and, because of this, it's easy to understand. It has four separate frequency bands. Here are the parameters you need to make it work.

Crossover; these three controls define the frequency ranges the bands will work over. The settings in Figure 5.34 are a good starting point.

- The compressor in band 1 will compress the frequency range 20Hz to 200Hz.
- The compressor in band 2 will compress the frequency range 200Hz to 800Hz.
- The compressor in band 3 will compress the frequency range 800Hz to 3200Hz.
- The compressor in band 4 will compress the frequency range 3200Hz to 220050Hz.
- The Threshold controls act in the same way as on a single Channel Compressor. Bringing the Threshold level down increases the compression effect.

Info

As usual with EQ, you need to adjust parameters while using your ears. You can't really 'see' an EQ!

Figure 5.34

The headroom controls are used to make up the gain lost when you pull the threshold controls down.

Start by listening to the audio and try and gauge where the problems are. Do you need more consistency in the level of the mid range? Are the high frequencies too prominent? Look at the meters at the bottom of the window. These will give you an idea of the overall balance.

Figure 5.35

If you feel that one of the frequency ranges sounds wrong, try adjusting the Threshold and Headroom controls for that frequency. Remember: bringing down the Threshold increases the compression, evening out the sound and you'll probably need to increase the Headroom slider to compensate.

The Attack Time controls adjust how fast the compression happens – i.e. how long it takes to turn the level down. If this is set to a high value, transients will pass through before the compressor has time to react.

The Release Time controls how fast the signal returns to its normal level. Setting too slow a release time will cause a 'pumping' effect – which can be a good thing in some circumstances.

Info

If you are using a Multiband compressor to master, try looking at the EQ curve of a song you like the sound of by inserting a Channel EQ and using the Analyzer (or the Multimeter) to see the EQ curve. You can then insert a Channel EQ on the master output after the Multi band compressor so you can see the effect the Multiband is having on the sound.

The MultiPressor

This is a more sophisticated Multiband compressor (Figure 5.37), but it works in the same way as the AUMultiBand compressor. You can set the Compression ratio, Attack, Release and Threshold separately for each band. To use it you select the number of bands you wish to use (Figure 5.38). The frequency range over which each band works is chosen by dragging the

Figure 5.37

Figure 5.38

sides of the bands (Figure 5.39). Select a band, adjust the controls for that band (Figure 5.40), then select another band and repeat.

Figure 5.39

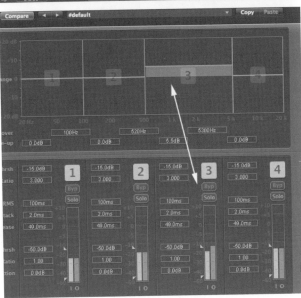

Figure 5.40

The MultiPressor has a few extra controls:

Compression ratio: this sets the amount of gain reduction for each band. A ratio of 4:1 will reduce the level of the signal by 1db for every 4dB it goes over the Threshold level.

Threshold: this sets the minimum level at which the compressor starts to work. Signals below this level wont be compressed.

Lookahead: using a small lookahead value lets the MultiPressor react earlier to sudden peaks, This feature adds latency, but that shouldn't be a problem if you're using it with full PDC or on the Master output channel.

Peak/RMS: use RMS detection when you're compressing music.

Expander: this feature lowers the level under a set Threshold. It's the opposite of compression and is useful for lowering the noise floor.

Tip

Keep an eye on the meters to see and balance the individual frequency ranges.

Reduction: you can use this control to lower the noise floor level. Compression inevitably increases the noise in a recording.

Resizing plug-in windows

Logic Pro's own plug-ins can be resized either by dragging the bottom right of the window or using the View menu. Many plug-ins have hidden parameters revealed by clicking on the arrow at the bottom of the plug-in window.

Figure 5.38

Figure 5.39

Workflow

This chapter has some tips that will allow you to speed up your workflow when using Logic – and make it more pleasing to the eye!

Customising how Logic looks

Not everyone likes the default look of Logic. There are a few ways to change the way things look.

Customising the Arrange page

In Logic Pro 9, the Arrange page has several features that cannot be changed, such as the Toolbar and editor tabs. However, nearly everything else can be modified.

If you're using a small screen and need the maximum screen space for Tracks you can hide the Transport bar or Toolbar using the Arrange page

Figure 6.2

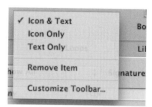

View menu>Transport or Toolbar menu items. You can hide the Inspector using the Arrange page View menu>Inspector menu item. You can hide the Media browser using the Arrange page View menu>Inspector menu item.

You can decide what is displayed on the Toolbar by right or CTRL clicking on the bar. A window opens where you can add or remove various items (Figures 6.2 and 6.3).

You can decide what is displayed on the Transport bar by right or CTRL clicking on the bar. A window opens where you can add or remove various items.

Figures 6.3 and 6.4

Figure 6.5

Double clicking on the CPU on the Transport bar will open the traditional CPU monitor.

The Display Preferences

The Display Preferences *General window*

Large local windows. If you are using a high resolution monitor or working at a distance, you can increase the size of the menus in the windows.

Wide Playhead. This can be easier to see on some screens, especially laptop screens.

Show help tags. When you drag a Region or Note a small text box appears with positional information. It can be in the way in some cases, so you can turn it off here.

Show default values. This show or hides the values displayed in the Region Parameter box.

Figures 6.6 – 6.8

The Display Preferences *Arrange window*

Background colour. You can choose between the mausoleum-dark default Arrange page background or a more cheery light one. You can choose your own from the Custom menu – if you double click on the colour box a colour picker will open (Figure 6.9).

Figure 6.9

The Display Preferences' Mixer Window

In this window you can set the default size of plug-in windows and the way the level meters respond.

The Display Preferences' Piano Roll Window

In this window you can change the appearance of the Piano roll editor window.

Figure 6.9a

Figure 6.10 (right)

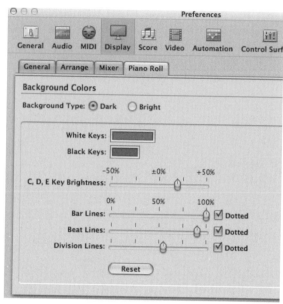

Using colours

You can use colours to keep a track of various Regions in a Arrange page.

Colouring Takes when using Quick Swipe

See the section on Takes in Chapter 4 for more details

Setting a Track to a specific colour

Either choose a Track with no Regions on it or select the Track itself (and thus all Regions). From the Arrange page View menu, select Colors. A colour picker window opens and you can select a suitable

Figure 6.11 (right)

colour. Any new Regions created on that Track will have the same colour.

You can colour most objects in Logic. You may want to colour similar Environment objects or all the hi-hat notes in the Piano roll (Matrix) editor.

Instrument names in the Arrange page

You can choose how to name your Tracks by using the Configure Track Header parameters. Right or CTRL click on the Track name to open the window. You can select how you want the track names to appear.

- Track name displays the Name you have given the Track by double clicking on its name.
- Channel Strip – displays the name of the selected Channel strip
- Software Instrument displays the name of the selected Instrument
- Automatic Track Name: This option (the default) intelligently names the track, based on the following actions, and order:

    * If you enter a track name manually, the track name is displayed.
    * If you loaded a channel strip setting or software instrument, the name of the channel strip setting or software instrument is displayed.
    * If you did none of the above, the channel strip name is displayed.

If you can't see the Instrument name box, drag the Track column to the right. If you click on the tick box in the Names section another Name section opens on the Track list. This has the same options as above and allows you to have two visible reminders what of what a Track is actually playing back.

Figures 6.12 and 6.13

Figure 6.14

Figure 6.15

If you double click on the Track name you can enter a description that will also appear in the mixer (Figure 6.15).

Using Icons

Each Object in Logic can have an Icon associated with it. If you select a Track in the Arrange page or an object in the Environment, you'll see the icon associated with it in the Track parameter box.

Figure 6.16

You can change the Icon by holding the mouse button on it in the Inspector. A list opens. Choosing a suitable Icon can make finding Tracks in a busy Arrange page easier.

You can use custom Icons in Logic. They are stored in the /Library/Application Support/Logic/Images/Icons folder. This folder isn't created by default. The Icon filenames should be xxx.png, where xxx is a 1 to 3 digit number. The Icons are 128x128 in size, must have an Alpha Channel for transparency and be saved in the Portable Graphics Format (.png) which most graphics software can export.

Tip

You should choose an icon filename of 326.png or above. Numbers 1-325.png are reserved for Logic's default Icons.

Window menu Transport bar

The Transport in the Window menu is particularly flexible. You can change its size and shape and have only portions of the Transport available. As you can have as many Transports open as you want, you can completely customize your Screensets.

Figure 6.17

- Use a very large Transport or SMPTE counter if you are working away from the screen. Right or CTRL click on the position display to see the options.
- Select what is displayed on the Transport bar from the Configuration menu – right or CTRL click on the Transport to see it.
- Transport layouts are stored in Screensets.
- Right or CTRL clicking and holding on some of the Transport bar buttons brings up various menus related to Transport functions. Right is the metronome settings pull-down menu.

Click While Recording
Click While Playing

Metronome Settings...

Scroll in play

Normally, Logic moves the playhead as a Song plays. However, you can change this behaviour. If you select Scroll in Play from the Arrange page View menu, the playhead will now remain static at the centre of the screen and the Regions will scroll by. You turn it on from the Arrange page View menu. This feature requires a powerful computer and video card to work smoothly.

Zooming in Logic

Although you can set up different Screensets in Logic with different Zoom levels, many people prefer to work in a single window. You can use the Zoom controls at the bottom of a window, or use the mouse (as detailed in Chapter 3), but sometimes this is inconvenient

and time consuming – and the mouse may not be at hand. Logic has several automatic zoom and Key Command functions related to Zoom.

Automatic track zooming

You can switch this on from the Arrange page View menu. Then, when you select a Track it is zoomed out with respect to all other Tracks.

Zooming individual Tracks

If you move the mouse to the bottom left of a Track, the cursor changes to a finger. You can then zoom each Track individually.

Zoom Key Commands

Using the zoom Key Commands is a handy way of changing the layout of a Logic screen. You may want to enlarge a Track so you can see where a waveform or MIDI data starts or ends or to check the lining up of Regions, then zoom back out to see an overview. The 'Recall Zoom' and 'Save as Zoom' Key Commands are particularly useful here for this (Figure 6.22).

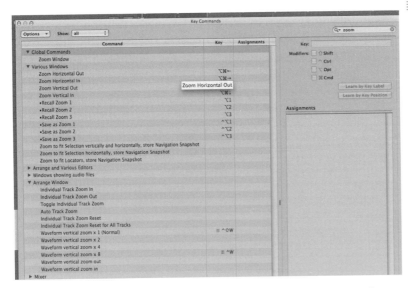

Figure 6.22

Use the 'Waveform vertical Zoom' icon to see more of an audio waveform – this is particularly useful for editing audio in the Arrange page.

Figures 6.23 and 6.24

Zoom navigation history

Logic stores the last 30 zoom and scroll positions of open windows. You can navigate backwards and forwards though this navigation history using the Navigation: Back and Navigation: Forward Key Commands.

Process buffers

These somewhat mysterious buffers are located in the Audio Preferences Core Audio Drivers window. It's worth experimenting with this value. It usually defaults to Medium.

- A small Process Buffer can improve the responsiveness of Logic. It does however require more processing power – so you may get dropouts or other processing errors.
- A large Process Buffer reduces the amount of processing power required to run Logic. However, it will increase latency and may make Logic feel less responsive.

Figure 6.26

SMPTE Time ruler

The default ruler at the top of the Arrange and Editor pages is in Bars. You can add a SMPTE absolute time display using the menu on the right of the window. Bar and Time displays both Bar and SMPTE. You may want to do this if you're working to picture.

You can choose the format of the display from the Display Preferences General window.

Using markers to display lyrics

You can use Logic as a kind of 'teleprompter' and display lyrics as it plays by using Markers. First set up some Markers. You need one Marker per lyric section. For example, you may want to display each couplet as it comes along.

Figure 6.27

- Create some Markers at the position in the Song you want the lyric to change open the Marker list window (Figure 6.27).
- Double click on a Marker and a text editor opens. Type in the lyric. Choose the font and size.
- Double click on the next marker and repeat the process.

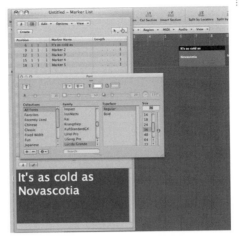

Tip

Use the Create Marker Key Command to easily create markers at the playhead.

Once all the lyrics are input, close the marker list window. Now select the Options>Marker>Open Marker Text window. Align and resize as necessary. Make sure the Running Man icon is ON (right) so the text editor changes as the Song progresses.

Now as you play the song, the text in the window will change at the required point.

Figure 6.28

Exporting tracks and Regions as audio files

You may want to convert whole tracks of audio or Virtual instruments, or Regions on a track to audio files for re-importing into Logic or for sending off to a colleague who is using another DAW. Use the File>Export menu to do this. This method of exporting saves files with all the automation and plug-in processing. It's like freezing, but you can choose which file format to use (Figure 6.30). You can then drag the exported files back into Logic.

Info

This technique is really useful if you wish to collaborate with someone who doesn't use Logic – perhaps they are using Pro Tools or Cubase? If you export all the Tracks, all your collaborator has to do is to load in all the audio files and line them up at the start. If you want to archive a recording (in case your DAW or plug-ins are not available in the future) or your collaborator wishes to get the audio 'raw', that is without being processed by plug-ins, you'll have to bypass all of the plug-ins and disable automation and set all the Pan and Volume controls to '0' (Option-click on a control to do this). Don't forget to do this with any Auxes and Busses too. Make sure you export the files in the format your collaborator can use. See Chapter 4 for more on file formats.

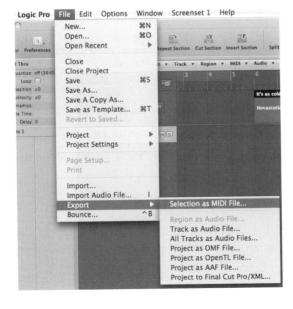

Figure 6.30

Environment tips

Layers

Logic's Environment can seem complicated and can contain a lot of objects all cabled together. It makes sense to keep related objects on separate pages or Layers. You could, for example, have a Layer containing an editor for a synthesizer, another for Audio objects, another for the Auxes that a multiple output virtual Instrument is cabled to.

Figure 6.31

Figures 6.32 and 6.33

Layers are created by clicking and holding on the Layer box. You can also select Layers here (Figure 6.32). Layers are named by double clicking on the Layer name (Figure 6.33). Layers appear in the pull-down menus in the Arrange page instrument Tracks (Figure 6.34).

Figure 6.34

Environment objects

The Environment contains many useful objects that are used to modify the flow of MIDI data. You can use these with external MIDI equipment or Virtual Instruments.

Using the Arpeggiator

Logic has a rather nifty Arpeggiator. Here's how you set it up and use it. Open the Environment and create a new Page. Call it Arpeggiators (right).

Create an Arpeggiator object from the Environment page New menu. Hold down the Option key and click on the little arrow on the Arpeggiator object. You can now cable the Arpeggiator to the required sound source. In this example, it's cabled to Instrument object 1 which has an ES1 running on it. Hold down the Option key and click on the little arrow at the top right of the Arpeggiator.

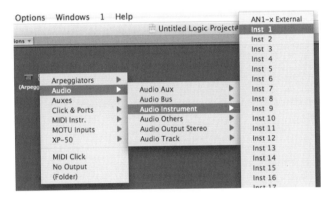

Figure 6.36

Select the Arpeggiator object. You'll see in the Parameter box the different parameters that can be used with the Arpeggiator. Make sure the box next to the icon is ticked. Rename it to something useful and give it a nice icon (right).

To use the Arpeggiator, select it in the Arrange page and put Logic into play. The Arpeggiator only works when Logic is running. Play some notes and chords to hear the effect and change Arpeggiator parameters to hear their effect. Then use the 'Capture last take' Key Command to record the results.

Info

When bouncing down a Song with Arpeggiators you must use Real Time bouncing.

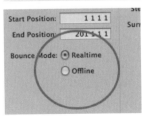

Figures 6.37 and 6.38

The Transformer

Using controller pedals in Logic

A lot of software these days, especially orchestral plug-ins, make use of MIDI controller data in an attempt to improve the realism of a performance. They may for example, use the Expression MIDI control change message (cc11) to adjust vital aspects of volume and timbre. If you are using an expression pedal into a master keyboard you can often set-up the keyboard to determine which MIDI control number is output into Logic when you move the pedal. However, when you are running several different plug-ins with different MIDI controller number requirements it can become inconvenient to keep reselecting the correct one on the master keyboard. You can use Logic's Environment to make this easier to manage.

Open the Environment and create a new layer. Create two Monitors, an Instrument and Transformer object. Cable and rename them as shown in Figure 6.40. If you then Option/Click on the little arrow on the second

Figure 6.40

Monitor object, you can cable this to your plug-in – in this case, the GPO, which is inserted on Audio Instrument 2.

Double click on the Transformer object and enter the parameters as in Figure 6.42. If you now select the Instrument ('GPO Controller 11') in the Arrange page and move the foot pedal, the required MIDI cc will be sent to GPO. As you can see from the last figure, the transformer is converting MIDI cc 4 to MIDI cc 11.

Figures 6.41 and 6.42

Multi Instruments and MIDI patch names

Using Multi-timbral external hardware synthesisers in Logic

You'll need to use the Environment to create a Multi Instrument object that you can use with the external Mutli Timbral synthesizer.

From the New menu, create a multi-instrument and drag it to the top left of the Environment window. Make sure there is not a tick in the box next to Icon in the Parameter box for this object. Rename the object to the real name of your MIDI device by highlighting it and double clicking on the name in the Parameter box – 'Multi Instr.' (Figure 6.43). Now select the port the MIDI device is connected to using the pull down menu on the Parameter list (Figure 6.44).

Info

A multi-timbral synthesizer is one that can play back many different sounds on up to 16 (or 32) different MIDI channels.

Figures 6.43 and 6.44

Click on the '1' on the Multi instrument so it is uncrossed and highlighted. This selects the sub-instrument that will use MIDI channel 1 on your synthesiser. Click on the box next to Program, so the instrument will receive program changes. Make sure the box next to Icon is crossed too so you can select it in the Arrange page. Notice that the Parameter box changes as well. It now displays the Parameters for the sub-channel rather than the whole multi-instrument object (Figure 6.45). Now open an Arrange page. You can select the Roland XP50 MIDI channel '1' from the pull down menu in the Track Column. Notice that the Environment layers are shown here too. Select

Figures 6.45 and 6.46

'Roland XP 1 Grand Piano' from the 'Synths' layer. Play a note on your MIDI keyboard. You should hear sound out of your synthesiser. It probably won't be Grand Piano sound though! (Figure 6.46).

If you don't hear a sound, check the following:

Make sure all your MIDI cables are connected correctly and your synthesizer is connected to an amplifier or headphones. Check the Audio MIDI Setup application from the Applications/Utilities folder and check that your MIDI interface is connected.

When you press your MIDI keyboard, do you see values appearing in the IN and OUT boxes on the transport bar (left)? If there are no IN values, check the connections between the MIDI OUT and MIDI IN on your computer. If there are no OUT values make sure you have set the correct port in the Multi-instrument and the MIDI cables.

To set up the next channel, click on the '2' on the Multi instrument so it is uncrossed and highlighted. Click on the box next to Program, so the instrument will receive program changes. Make sure the box next to Icon is crossed too.

Figure 6.48

Repeat this for all 16 MIDI channels if you require them. The pull-down menu on the Arrange page should now look something like Figure 6.49. Of

Figure 6.49

course all the sounds on the Roland XP50 aren't Grand Pianos! Fortunately, Logic provides a way to name all the patches that actually are loaded into your synthesiser. You can then select these by name, rather than just a choosing a patch number. Double click on the top of the Multi Instrument. This will open a patch name box (Figure 6.50). Of course these default names are unlikely to be the ones on your synthesiser, so you'll have to rename them appropriately.

Select bank 0 from the pull down menu (Figure 6.51). Your synthesiser may need special bank change parameters. You'll need to look in the manual of your MIDI device, and select the appropriate Bank Message from the menu. Now delete all the names in the window by choosing 'Cut all names' from the pull down menu (Figure 6.52).

Figure 6.50

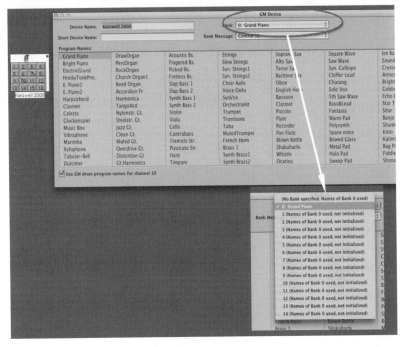

Figure 6.51

Now you can type in the names of the patches on your synthesiser. Double click on each of the boxes in turn and type in the correct name of the patch. When you have finished typing in all the names in a bank, change to the next bank. Logic will initialize it for you, and then you can continue to enter patch names.

Figures 6.52 and 6.53

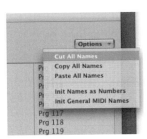

As you can imagine, it can take quite a while to type in patch names on a synthesiser that has 16 banks of 128 sounds! Luckily you can copy the patch names from either a patch editor or another Logic song that has the names of the patches for your synthesisers already entered. You can find a lot of Logic songs containing this sort of thing on the Internet. See Appendix 3 for more details.

Project information

Figure 6.54

This feature can be found in the main Options menu. It gives various useful information about your Song. The Reorganize menory button can help if you are having problems running your Song.

MIDI reset

If you get hung MIDI notes, you can reset the MIDI interface by double-clicking on the In/Out section of the Transport.

Bounce in place – render in place

If you have a Virtual Instrument you'd like to render or bounce to an audio file, to send to a colleague without Logic, for example or an audio Region packed with effects that's taxing your CPU, you can bounce just that Region to disk. Right or CTRL clicking on a Region and selecting Bounce in place opens a window (Figure 6.55).

You can choose to leave, mute or delete the original – choose mute if you think you may want to edit the associated Track's processing further. You'd

Info

Use the Bypass Effect Plug-ins if you want to bounce a 'raw' audio file – for using in a sample or collaboration with others. You can also choose to ignore automation and pan in the bounce.

normally create the bounced Region on a new Track. For example, if you only want to permanently process a single Region on a Track, you'd want to mute the original Region (Figure 6.56).

Normalize would usually be used if you want to use the Region for drum replacement – all the usual caveats for normal-izing audio (higher noise floor) apply here.

The Add Effects Tail to File checkbox bounces to the end of

Info

You can bounce all the Regions in all Tracks from the Arrange page Bounce Replace all Tracks accessible from the Track menu.

Figure 6.55

Figure 6.56

the cycle or to the end of the last selected region or until the audio runs out until there is no longer a signal, while the Add Effects Tail to Region checkbox includes the entire bounce file in the bounce region. Un-clicked, only the range between the locators is bounced. Both of these can be used if you're losing the end of an effect, e.g. reverb or echo from the resulting bounce.

If you're using a multi-output Virtual Instrument, such as EXS24 or Ultrabeat, Bounce in Place will create individual bounces from each output if you select the option in the Bounce window (Figure 6.57).

Confusingly though it bounces them all to a stereo file. If you want separate Regions for each output, you need to solo the Auxes that the separate outputs are routed through in turn. Each Bounce in place will then create a Region or Track only for that Aux. In the figure below, Ultrabeat's output from 5 and 6 only are bounced (Figure 6.58).

Figures 6.57 and 6.58

Quickly creating Tracks

If you Alt click on the Create Track button, a Track is created of the same type as the current one

Figure 6.59

Figure 6.60 and 6.61

Finding the hidden main window Transport bar features

CTRL or right clicking on the buttons on the Transport bar reveals various useful menus relating to that specific button. For example, the Cycle bar allows you to set various ways to set Locators (Figure 6.60).

While the Record button allows you set the various recording options (Figure 6.61).

You can add or remove Transport bar features using the Customize Transport window, acessible from by right or CTRL clicking on the Transport bar (Figure 6.62).

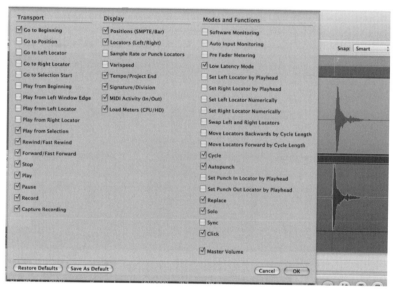

Figure 6.62

Making notes – keeping track of Tracks and Projects

Track notes

While Markers are useful for keeping notes on a Project, Logic Pro 9 now has 'scribble strips' at the bottom of the Mixer page called Notes. Turn these on and off from the Mixer's View menu or the small icon at the bottom of the Mixer (Figure 6.63). Here, you could type information about the instrument, how it was recorded and so on. Scribble areas can be resized and right or CTRL clicking on them, brings up several text editing features (Figures 6.64 and 6.65).

Figure 6.63 and 6.64

Figure 6.65

Project notes

You can add notes for the whole Project, such as location, band information or anything useful to the Project. You open Project Notes from the icon on the main Toolbar.

Editing is enabled by the pencil icon, while clicking on the A brings up further text editing options (Figure 6.66). You can also edit Track notes here using the editing options. Select which icons appear on the Toolbar by right or CTRL clicking on them. A window opens up where you can choose the Tools displayed.

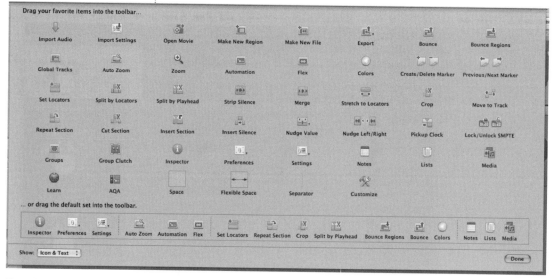

Figure 6.66

Selective import of tracks from a different Project

You can import tracks from a saved Project directly into the current one by opening the Media browser (Figure 6.67).

Figure 6.67

Figure 6.68

Clicking on the Project icon (Figure 6.68), and finding the Project you wish to import from (Figure 6.69).

Figure 6.69

Double clicking on the Project in the Browser opens the Import window (Figure 6.70). You can select which part of a Track to Import.

- Content (the actual audio or MIDI data on a Track)
- Inserted plug-ins (listed here)
- Sends
- Inputs and outputs (i/o)
- Automation

Figure 6.70

Once selected you can add or Replace Tracks in the current Project.

You can also Import other Project settings by clicking on the Import Project Settings button, and selecting the required data to be Imported from the window (Figure 6.71).

Figure 6.71

The Arrange page, Editor windows and more editing tips

General editing tips

Working with Regions

Holding the Option key while cutting a Region with the Scissors tool will split it into equal slices.

Figure 7.1

Removing overlaps

When you record MIDI data in real time it's likely you'll get notes overlapping.

Figure 7.2

These notes can cause problems with Drum plug-ins and monophonic lines. You can get rid of these overlaps in the Piano Roll (Matrix) and List editors by selecting the notes and using the Functions>Note Events overlap correction menu items.

Figure 7.3

Removing duplicates

In a similar fashion, any doubles notes can be removed using the Editor's Function>Delete MIDI events>Duplicates menu item.

Inputs and outputs

In certain editors, the following icons are available. They deal with the input and output of MIDI data.

When on, 'IN' allows MIDI data to be input via an external MIDI device. When 'OUT' is on, clicking on an event outputs it to your MIDI devices.

Default editor window

You can set which tabbed editor window opens when you double-click on a MIDI Region from the Global Preferences Editing window.

The tabbed Sample editor will always open when you double-click on an Audio Region in Logic Pro 9 – unlike earlier versions where you could assign floating editor windows.

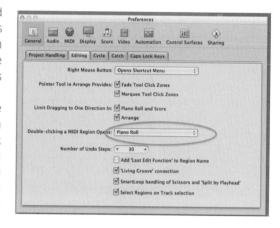

Selecting events in the Editors

Alongside the selection criteria in a window's Edit menu, some editors have Function menus that have select options in their Note Events menu. This is from the Piano Roll editor.

Figure 7.7

- Selecting Top Line is useful for extracting the melody line from a chordal keyboard part.
- Selecting Bottom Line is useful for extracting the bass line from a chordal keyboard part.

Using Key Commands in the Arrange page and Editors

There are several Key Commands associated with each editor, which can help in selecting and moving around.

Select First/last/Previous and Next Event. These Key Commands allow you to quickly navigate the Regions in the Arrange page and notes in the other Editors.

Select inside Locators and Deselect outside Locators. These commands make it easy to delete or copy whole sections of a Song.

Select Muted Regions. This Key Command is used to select (then remove) muted Regions you may not be using in a Song.

Select First/last/Previous and Next Track. Use these Key Commands in the Arrange page to help move around using the computer keyboard.

Select First/last/Previous and Next Region. Use these Key Commands in the Arrange page to help move around using the computer keyboard.

Hyperdraw in the Arrange page and the Editing windows

Hyperdraw is Logic's older Region based automation system. For more general automation, you'll probably want to use Logics more accurate Track-based system. But it's still useful for these reasons.

- It can be used to draw MIDI controller curves
- It can be used for fine editing of volume and controllers on a per-region basis.

Hyperdraw is a way of drawing controller information directly on the Regions themselves. You can draw any controller information but the most useful are obviously volume, pan, modulation, aftertouch and pitchbend.

Open the Piano Roll or Score Editors. Make the Hyperdraw area visible from the View Hyperdraw menu.

Choosing a Hyperdraw controller

Either select a controller from the View>Hyperdraw menu, or click on the small arrow at the left of the Hyperdraw window and choose a controller from there. For this example, choose controller 7 (Volume). Now click on the region to draw a Hyperdraw curve. At each click, a MIDI Volume (controller number 7) event (node) is created and a line drawn between them. Events can be dragged and moved at will.

Moving the whole curve

Holding down the Option while you drag a Hyperdraw event, moves all the Hyperdraw nodes to the right of the node you click on.

Deleting individual Hyperdraw events

Click on each event to delete it. The line is re-drawn between the nearest two events.

Deleting all the Hyperdraw events

Hold down the Option key and double click on a node to delete all the events.

Finer editing of Hyperdraw events

Highlight the region. Open the Event List editor. Make sure just the controller data icon is on and the Note icon is OFF. This will ensure only controller events are displayed. You can see and edit all the nodes you have just created (Figure 7.10).

Figure 7.10

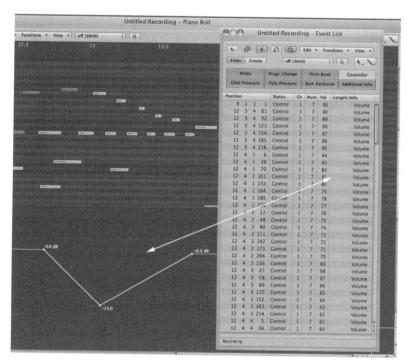

Tip

You can bring to the front and re-edit the previous Volume Hyperdraw events by choosing the View > Hyperdraw > Volume menu item.

If you want to draw the curve for a different controller number, let's say Pan (controller number 10), select it from the View>Hyperdraw>menu item. The volume data curve on the region is greyed out. You can now draw on the Region in the same fashion as for the volume curve.

Hyperdraw can be useful with Virtual instruments that use unusual controllers. Some orchestral libraries use multiple controllers to help produce a realistic result – they may control timbre, volume, vibrato, bow strokes and so on.

The Hyper editor

Using the Hyper editor as a drum editor

Logic does not have a dedicated drum editor. As it is sometimes useful when editing drum parts to see the notes on a grid, you can use the Hyper editor to perform this function. The easiest way to set up a hyperset as a drum editor is as to create a mapped instrument of your drum and percussion sounds.

How to set up a Mapped instrument

In the Environment window select the New>Mapped Instrument menu item. A window will open. Close it. Move the Mapped instrument to a convenient place.

In our example, the Mapped instrument would control an Alesis D4 drum module, but it could just as easily be any Virtual instrument, drum machine or sound on a Multi timbral synth.

Highlight the mapped instrument and change the MIDI channel to 10 in the Cha field in the Parameter box. While it's Highlighted, rename it, make sure there is a cross in the box next to the Icon in the Parameter box and make sure you can see the cables from the View>Cables menu item. Set the Port: to OFF – this mapped instrument will only be used to control the Alesis D4 drum module.

Figures 7.11 – 7.13

Cable the Mapped instrument to the Alesis D4 Multi by dragging the cable from the little arrow at the top right. If the Instrument object is on another Environment page, hold down the Option key when you click and choose it from the pull down menu. Remove the channel port setting when asked by Logic (Figure 7.13). Rename the Mapped instrument to something useful – 'Alesis D4Mapped Instrument' (Figure 7.14).

Figure 7.14

If you look in the instrument menu on the track column in the Arrange page you will see the Mapped instrument. Select it and check it plays your drum sounds.

Figure 7.15

If you want the Mapped instrument to play a Virtual plug-in (such as Ultrabeat or the EXS24 sampler, cable the Mapped instrument to the Audio object the Virtual instrument is on. Remove the channel port setting when asked by Logic.

Figure 7.16

We'll use this connection to create the Mapped instrument. Double click on the Mapped instrument to open the window again (Figure 7.17). The window has the following properties:

- Click on the keyboard to the left of the window; it will play the sounds assigned to that key.
- Double click on the name of a drum sound to change it.

Figure 7.17

Figure 7.18

You can then give each drum (or key) its own name.

Figure 7.19

Open the Hyperedit window and record a short sequence using all the sounds assigned to keys. Just click on the pause and record button on the transport bar (or select record via a key command) and play each note in turn. No need to press play. Then stop recording. Remember; don't press play!

Make sure the sequence is selected and then open the Hyper editor. Select HYPER>CREATE HYPER SET menu item. Double click on 'set initialized' and enter a useful name, Like 'Ultrabeat drums 1'

Click on the volume event definition and select the HYPER>DELETE EVENT DEFINITION menu item.

Select the HYPER>MULTI CREATE EVENT DEFINITION menu item. In the Dialog box which appears, select ALL (all events in current sequence). You will see something like Figure 7.20.

Figure 7.20

The names of the drums down the left of the window are imported from your Mapped instrument. Select the EDIT>SELECT ALL menu item. Press the delete key to delete the drum events, i.e. the notes you played in. Adjust the zoom of the window as desired.

You can now enter drum data directly with the pencil tool or by recording as usual from the MIDI keyboard (you may want to switch the File>Song settings>Recording>Merge new recordings with selected regions menu item to ON, if you want to loop around and add new notes at each pass. Step time input is also useful when writing drum parts – see Chapter 4 for more on this.

You can delete notes with the eraser tool and drag them around as with any events in Logic. You can also change the grid values for each event definition.

If you want to adjust the grid value of several event definitions, just Shift click on them to select them all. Grid values are changed in the Parameter box. You may want the bass drum (Kick 1) to default to 1/8th note, the Open HH to 1/16, so select these individually and edit the Grid parameter.

Info

The Grid value defines where new notes will appear on the Hyper edit window when you create them with the pencil tool. It's a sort of pre-quantize effect. For example, if you want to add a bass drum on every bar, change the grid value to 1:1. You can then only pencil in notes on the first beat of the bar. If you want to create hi-hats on every 16th beat, set the grid value to 1/16. Now, dragging the pencil across the Hyper editor, will create a hi-hat note on every 16th beat. You can, of course, change the grid value after you have drawn events. Grid values are changed in the Parameter box.

Figure 7.21

The velocities of the notes are shown as the dark areas of the note columns. These can be edited with the pencil tool. Note how easy it is to draw a variable velocity on the 'Tite HH' in Figure 7.21. Also notice the rise in the GatedSnare toward bar 9 (Figure 7.22).

Figure 7.22

Speaking of Hi Hats, next to the Hi Hats in the 'Drum Editor' in the next figure are some little dots with lines through them. These mean that these channel definitions are in 'Hi Hat mode' (just click to the left of the name to switch it on or off). What this means is that only one event can be output at the same time when in this mode. You may want this to happen if you are trying to emulate a human drummer more closely – only closed or open hi-hats can be played on one set at a time Figure 7.23).

Figure 7.23

Of course, you can group any instruments like this. You may want a monophonic bass line for example. The Hyper editor isn't just for drum notes!

Time stretching and tempo adjustment in the Arrange page

When you record MIDI data you can change the tempo of a song at will. However, any audio files (that are not Apple loops) will not change tempo. What you need is some way of stretching an audio region to fit the new Tempo. Luckily, Logic can do this. Here's the original recording of audio and MIDI at the original tempo of 120bpm.

Figure 7.24

If you change the tempo to 130bpm, the MIDI data changes along with Logic, but the audio doesn't (Figure 7.25).

Figure 7.25

Tempo using Logic Pro 8 or later

If an audio Region is recorded or imported into Logic Pro, clicking on the Follow Tempo box in the Region Inspector will allow the Audio to be stretched or compressed as you change the tempo along with any MIDI data. This uses the algorithms described later in the Chapter.

Figure 7.25a

Figure 7.25b

Using Flex mode to edit the tempo of audio files

See Chapter 4 for more information on Logic Pro 9's fluid audio tools.

You can also change the tempo of audio using the options in the Arrange page Audio menu (Figures 7.26 and 7.27).

Figures 7.26 and 7.27

Time stretch length to Locators

To use this feature, first set the locators to the bar length you require. In this case, you could select the MIDI file and use the 'Set Locators by Region' Key Command to set the locators. Now select the audio Region and choose the Arrange page>Audio>Adjust Region length to Locators menu item, to fit the audio to the tempo.

Time stretch Region length to nearest bar

This is similar to the Adjust Region length feature, but adjusts the audio Region tempo to the nearest bar. In this case the result would be identical.

The quality and type of the time stretching algorithm can be selected from the Audio menu. Note that in the figure two third-party algorithms are installed. The legacy ones are of inferior quality – but may be useful as an effect.

You can also time-stretch an audio recording by holding down the Option key and grabbing the bottom right of a Region. Logic will ask you if you want to compress or expand the region.

Figure 7.28

Figure 7.29

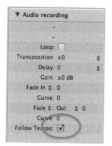

Figure 7.30

If you are using Logic 7 or greater, any audio recorded into Logic can automatically follow the tempo changes in a Song. You turn this feature on and off using the Track parameter box Follow Tempo: function (Figure 7.30). If this option is missing, it's because you have audio recorded in an earlier version of Logic. You can export and re-import this audio to allow it to follow tempo.

You can also stretch MIDI Regions to fit the Tempo of audio Regions using the Options>Tempo>Adjust Tempo using Region Length and Locators.

You can always UNDO the conversion and try another algorithm if the one you use isn't suitable.

You can also destructively adjust the length of an audio file without changing the pitch in the Time machine in the Sample editor.

Audio Regions are usually a small pointer to a part of a much larger audio file, other parts of which may be used in other parts of the Song or, indeed, other Songs. Use the Arrange page Audio Convert Regions to new audio files menu item to make sure that you are just editing the selected Region and don't accidentally edit the whole audio file a Region is part of.

You can time stretch MIDI Regions in the Arrange page by dragging the right hand side of the Region while holding down the Option key.

You can add third-party algorithms to Logic such as those from Izotope and Serato.

Arrange page tips

Adding audio files

You can add audio regions directly to the Arrange window in various ways. You need to select an Audio track for these to work.

- Hold down the shift key and click with the Pencil tool. That brings up the standard audio dialogue for opening files. The selected file will be added to the Audio window, and a Region will be placed at the mouse cursor on the Arrange page
- Drag audio files from the Finder onto the Arrange page or Audio bin directly. If you drag multiple files, they will be placed on consecutive tracks.
- Use the 'Import audio' Key Command.

Piano Roll editor tips

The Event Float

The Event float is a small editable window that displays information about any selected note or Region. You can open it from the View menu, but it makes more sense to assign it to the 'Open Event float' Key Command (Figure 7.31).

Hyperdraw

You can use Hyperdraw in the Piano Roll editor. It's selected from the View menu item.

Figure 7.31

Event List editor tips

You can have much of the same functionality in the Media inspector by selecting Lists from the Arrange page View menu.

Figure 7.32

Viewing events

Select which data is displayed from the icons in the editor (Figure 7.33):

- View, edit and add note data.
- View, edit and add program changes.
- View, edit and add Pitchbend data.
- View, edit and add Controller data.
- View, edit and add channel pressure – channel aftertouch.
- View, edit and add polyphonic pressure – polyphonic aftertouch.
- View, edit and add Systems exclusive data.
- View, edit and add Meta events (Additional info)

Notes		Progr. Change		Pitch Bend		Controller	
Chnl Pressure		Poly Pressure		Syst. Exclusive		Additional Info	
Position			Status	Ch	Num	Val	Length/Info
2	1	3 152	Note	2	G2	66	1 0 0 144
2	2	1 214	Note	2	C3	95	1 0 0 102
2	3	1 83	Note	2	A3	77	. . 3 171
2	3	4 154	Note	2	B3	86	. . 2 212
2	4	3 202	Note	2	E4	100	. 2 0 181
3	1	3 89	Note	2	F2	40	. 2 0 87
3	2	2 99	Note	2	G2	75	1 3 1 155
3	2	4 20	Note	2	C3	89	. 1 1 198
3	3	1 185	Note	2	D4	60	. . 3 81
3	3	3 107	Note	2	C4	17	. . 2 40
3	3	4 152	Note	2	B3	61	. . 1 131
3	4	1 99	Note	2	C2	68	. 1 2 100
3	4	1 220	Note	2	A3	61	. . 3 100
3	4	4 187	Note	2	C3	64	. 1 2 129
4	1	2 74	Note	2	A3	62	. . . 192
4	1	2 200	Note	2	B3	61	. . . 206
4	1	3 151	Note	2	C4	75	. . . 154
4	1	4 55	Note	2	A3	73	. . 3 224
4	1	4 162	Note	2	F2	39	. 3 3 64
4	2	3 120	Note	2	G3	77	. 1 0 181
4	3	2 55	Note	2	D3	14	. . 2 144
4	3	4 55	Note	2	F3	63	. 1 1 29
4	4	1 141	Note	2	C4	73	. . 2 133
4	4	3 18	Note	2	D2	82	. 1 0 167
5	1	1 59	Note	2	C3	75	. . 2 163
5	1	1 193	C–Press	2		59	
5	1	2 120	C–Press	2		0	
5	1	2 185	Note	2	F3	52	. . . 3 148
5	1	2 187	Note	2	B3	95	. . . 229
5	1	4 70	Note	2	A3	103	. . 1 152

Figure 7.33

Tip

Use a separate copy of the Song just for producing a score. Then, if you need to edit it, you'll still have the original copy.

Score editor tips

Just because a Song sounds good on playback, doesn't mean it will produce a playable score. Here are some tips that can help out. You'll probably want to do this in the Piano Roll editor.

Remove overlaps

If you have overlaps they can cause confusion in a score. Remove them by selecting all the notes in a Region and using the Piano Roll (Matrix) editor Functions>Note Events>Note event correction.

Remove doubles

In a similar fashion, you can remove any duplicate notes using the Functions>Erase MIDI events>Duplicates menu item.

Quantize

Use Logic's quantize menu to improve the appearance and playability of the score (Figure 7.34).

Figure 7.34

There are a few other Parameters you can use to improve your score output

Score Styles

As you can see from Figure 7.34, Logic has automatically picked up the fact that a piano was recorded and has split the stave into bass and treble. What has in fact happened is that Logic has chosen the default Score style 'Piano' in the display Parameter box.

Figure 7.35

If you hold and click on the Style Parameter, you can get a list of all the pre-defined score styles (Figure 7.36). Change them and see how they affect the score display.

If you want to edit a score style, double click on it in the display Parameter box; a window will open (Figure 7.37).

Here you can change the parameters of the score style. In most cases, the defaults can be left as they are, but all the parameters in the window can be edited with the mouse.

Figure 7.36

Figure 7.37

You may want to change:

- the *space* between staves
- the *TRP* or transpose values of the staves
- the *split* point of the staves

Display Quantization

As well as quantizing the actual MIDI data in the Piano Roll (Matrix) Editor, you can quantize the *display* of the notes in the Score Editor. The Default quantization is based on the display format from the Transport bar.

You may want to change the display quantization. There is a pop up menu displayed when you click and hold down the mouse key over the Quantize field (right). There are a collection of quantization values (such as 4, 8 etc.) and hybrid (4,3 etc.) values. The hybrid and higher resolution values work best where the original part is played with accuracy.

Figure 7.38

Interpretation

One of the most powerful features in Logic is its ability to suppress rests that may occur if a note is stopped short or played a little after the beat. This is toggled *on* and *off* from the Interpretation parameter in the display Parameter box. Here's a piano part with Interpretation set to *off*.

Figure 7.39

And here's the piano part with Interpretation set to ON.

Figure 7.40

Syncopation

When it is *on*, the notes are displayed as actual note values (Figure 7.41).

Figure 7.41

When this parameter is *off* syncopations are displayed as smaller note values tied across the beat (Figure 7.42).

Figure 7.42

No Overlap

When this is *on*, it suppresses the display of portions of notes, which overlap past the beginning of new notes. This is overlap *off*. Note all the spurious ties (Figure 7.43).

This is overlap set to *on*. You can normally leave this *on*.

Figure 7.43

Figure 7.44

Maximum dots

This sets the maximum number of dots that can be displayed after a note. The setting you choose depends on what you want your score to look like. If you don't know what to put in here, leave it set to 1.

Sample editor tips

Sample-accurate editing

To fine-tune the start and end point of an audio file at sample level resolution:

- Double click on the Region to open it in the Sample editor.
- You can change the Region start point by dragging the left arrow at the Region start flag. The Anchor point (the actual start of the audio in the Region) will also move (Figure 7.45).
- You can change the Region end point by dragging the arrow at the end of the Region (Figure 7.46).
- The Anchor point is the actual start of the Audio – it can be in a different place from the Region start and will move the audio in the Arrange page.

You can edit audio to sample accuracy directly on the Arrange page if you zoom in enough.

Figures 7.45 and 7.46

Other useful stuff in the Sample editor

- Use the Sample editor to destructively fade, silence and trim audio files.
- Use the Remove DC Offset function if you have 'thumps' in your audio.

Figure 7.47

- Use the Search Silence function to find gaps in a long audio files
- Use the Search Peak function to detect clipping in an audio file. It will pick up any peak that reaches 0dB.

Figure 7.48

Click zones – making Tools easier to use

You can make the Marquee tool appear whatever Tool is selected by hovering the mouse pointer at the bottom half of a Region if you have the tick box enabled in the Editing Preferences window.

Figure 7.49

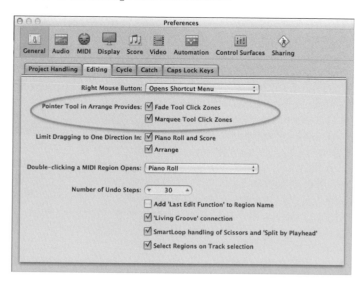

Similarly, you can make the Fade Tool appear by hovering in the top half of a Region if you have the tick box enabled.

Apple loops and fluid audio

Apple loops are specialized audio files that can easily be tempo matched to a song. Apple loops can also contain information about their content, making them searchable for content. Logic ships with many Apple loops and you can make your own using the supplied Apple loop utility. It's easier to see how Apple loops fit into the scheme of things within Logic by an example. The Loops browser is in the Media inspector (Figure 8.1).

If you have any Apple loops installed in the default location you'll see them displayed here. To audition an Apple loop click on it.

To add an Apple loop to a song, drag it to the Arrange page from the Loop browser (Figure 8.2). Now change the tempo in Logic. You'll hear that the audio in the Apple loops changes tempo too.

Apple loops have Tags associated with them. These tags provide information about the audio in the Apple loop, so you can use the search window in the browser and the scale and signature information to find the loops you need.

You can turn any Region into an Apple Loop by selecting it and using the Region>Add to Apple loops library menu item. A window will open where you can give the Loop a name and select the other tag which refer to the Loop.

Figure 8.1

Figure 8.2

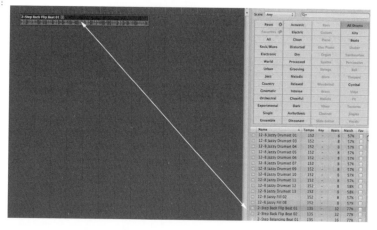

In this example, the Region is a drum loop and so we'll add All drums/Kits/Single/Dry tags (Figure 8.3). You can then select the Loop in the Loops bin under the My Loops menu (Figure 8.4).

Figures 8.3 and 8.4

 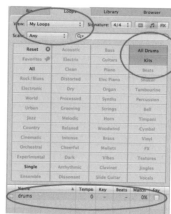

The Apple loops Utility

This is a separate program stored in the Applications folder. When you do this, Logic asks you to select a file to make into a Loop. Select a file and it will load into the application.

Figure 8.5 has an 8-bar drum Loop. Here, as an example, we can create an apple loop from a 8 bar recording of a drum kit. The original tempo is unknown. Once the file is loaded, you can fill in the Tag fields. In this example:

Number of beats =16
File type = looping
Key = none (as it's a percussion loop)
Scale= neither (as it's a percussion loop)
Time signature =4/4

Info

You can also load in an audio file. Click on the + in the file management (Assets) window. If it's not visible, click on the Assets button at the bottom left of the Apple Loops utility.

Figure 8.5

Set the Tags to the most useful for the Loop.

The Transients pane

In a percussion-based audio file, you may not know the tempo of the file. The transients pane can be used to determine tempo from the 'beats' in the file.

Figure 8.6

Tip

You can also use the BPM counter plug-in to determine an audio files tempo. Just insert it on the audio Track the Region you want to find the Tempo is on and press play.

You can fine-tune the Apple loops utility's beat detection using the following parameters:

Transient division

A high beat value (1/8th notes or less) will mean fewer transients being detected. This is useful for slow tempo recordings. A low beat value (1/6th notes or higher) will mean more transients being detected. This is useful for higher tempo recordings.

Sensitivity slider

This sets the amplitude or volume that the software will detect as being a transient. Low sensitivity means less transients being detected – i.e. only loud beats pass though.

Transients detected can be edited directly in the Transients pane. You can also add new transient information if the automatic system isn't suitable (for non- percussive audio files)

Adding a transient

Click in the area below the Transient division pull down menu.

Moving a transient

Drag the marker in the below the Transient division pull down menu.

Deleting a transient

Drag the marker out of the area below the Transient division pull down menu, or select it and press Delete. You can play back, and check out the effects of tempo changes of a created Apple loop.

Saving an Apple loop

Once you have created your loop, save it using the program's 'Save' button. To add it to Logic, just drag it from the Desktop to the Loop bin in Logic.

Mixing

These days, many users mix entirely 'In the box' – that is, without an external mixing console or even external effects. This chapter aims to provide tips and methodology that will help in the mixing process.

Mixer

This is heart of Logic. It's a visual representation of all the Tracks that are on the Arrange page. You can either open a separate Track mixer window from the Window menu or the Arrange page Tab.

Figure 9.1

You can can show and hide various Track types in the Mixer.

Creating Mixer Groups

The Track mixer shows all the Tracks on the Arrange page and it can get very big in horizontal direction in a large Song. You can create Track mixer 'groups' by using Folders in the Arrange page.

Choose the Arrange page menu item, Region>Folder>Pack Folder to create a folder in the Arrange page.

Figure 9.4

Double click on the Folder to open it. Create (or drag if you've already recorded something) the Tracks you want to have in a Group in the Folder.

Figures 9.5 and 9.6

Figure 9.7

Figure 9.8

In this example, it's all the audio Tracks used to play back a Guitar part. Close the Folder using the box at the top left of the Arrange page (Figure 9.5). Create another folder. This time it's for slide guitar (Figure 9.6).

Open the Mixer. Set the link button to Content Link (or double click it until it turns yellow.) (Figure 9.7). Now, when you double click on the Folder in the Arrange page, the Track mixer will change to reflect the Tracks in the Folder. Figure 9.8 shows the result of clicking on the Guitar folder and Figure 9.9 of clicking the slide guitar folder. Repeat for any other Track mixer configurations you require.

Grouping Track Mixer channels together

You may want to adjust the levels of some tracks together. You can group several objects together so that moving one of their faders will move all those in the same group and the same relative levels will be kept (Figure 9.10).

To assign a group to a Track, use the Group pull down menu (Figure 9.11).

Figure 9.9

Figure 9.10

Figure 9.11

Figure 9.12

You can see what group is selected on the Group display (Figure 9.12).

Figure 9.13

Info

Groups can be temporarily enabled and disabled by using a Key command. Disabling a group allows you to change the relative values of faders and so on in the group. Re-enabling the group re-instates the group movements. This is called the Group 'clutch'.

If you open the Group settings window (Figure 9.13) you can:

- Name the group (i.e. Drum 'Subgroup', 'Guitars' etc.)
- Choose what is to be grouped. For example, you could group sends to a bus (for reverb) or Arrange page automatic zooming as well as faders and pans.
- You can also temporarily group Tracks by holding down the Shift key and selecting Tracks.

Resetting parameters to default values and resetting faders to 0

You can reset any fader or pan pot (and most values in some plug-ins) to their default values by holding down the Option key and clicking on the control.

Dragging plug-ins

You can drag plug-ins around in the Track Mixer by selecting the hand tool (left) and dragging them to a new Track or another slot on the same Track. If you hold down the Option key you can copy the Plug-in along with all its settings. This is an easy way to set up similar plug-ins on several similar tracks.

Sends and busses (auxes)

In Logic 8 there's no distinction between auxes and busses. Logic routes audio to busses from Tracks but the sends and outputs appear as Auxes in the Mixer window.

If you have multiple Tracks, for example five drum Tracks, you may want to add a reverb to all of them to get a specific ambience, or put a compressor across the whole drum kit. Adding the same reverb and compressor to all the Tracks is possible but inefficient – it uses up a lot of CPU power. It's often better to use a single plug-in to process many Tracks rather than use an individual one on each Track. We can do this using a bus. You can either do this on individual Tracks in the Channel strip display or in the Mixer window. Here you can select several Tracks at once and send all their outputs or sends to the same bus (Figure 9.15).

Select the Track(s) you want to send audio to the bus from. In this example we have 5 drum tracks. Now select a bus from the output pull down menu.

Insert your effects plug-ins on the Aux (Figure 9.17). Create an Aux using the '+' icon and select the required bus as an input. In this example, choose bus 2.

Figure 9.15

Figure 9.17

You can see that the Aux chosen has bus 2 as its input (below left).

Give the Aux a useful name (right). Now the Audio from each Track is being routed to the bus and thus through the effects.

Info

If you want the Auxes to show up in the Arrange page, create a new Audio Track and right or CTRL click on the Track header to insert the Aux. You may want to do this if you want to Automate Auxes.

Bringing external hardware into Logic

Although it's possible to record and mix entirely in Logic using its own and third party plug-ins, many people want to use their old synthesisers and effects units too.

Live inputs and external hardware

If you have a soundcard or interface with multiple inputs, you can route the outputs from an external synthesiser or mixing desk back into Logic Pro. These inputs can then be incorporated with audio tracks and virtual instruments when bouncing down, eliminating the use of an external mastering machine, such as DAT or Tape.

Live inputs are just another Audio object. Here's how you use them in Logic.

- Create a new Environment layer for your inputs and create an Input object from the Environment page New>Channel strip menu item (right).
- Give it a useful name like 'DX7 input.

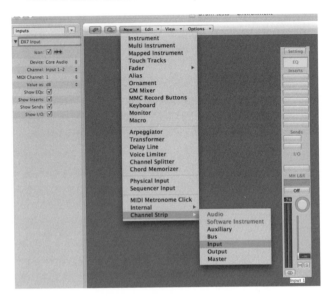

- On the Arrange page create a new Audio track from the '+' icon. Reassign it to an Input by right or CTRL clicking on the Track name. As you can see the Environment layer is visible with the Input object.

- Now choose a mono or stereo input from the Channel's input menu. These inputs represent the physical inputs on your interface. The examples here are inputs 13 and 14 (Figure 9.25).

Figure 9.25

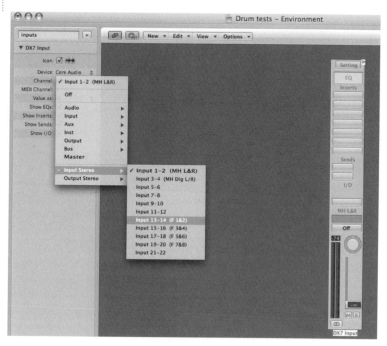

- If you are returning the sound from an effects unit, such as a reverb, you'll obviously need to send the audio to the unit from somewhere within Logic. The best way to do this is to use an Aux.
- On the Arrange page create a new Audio track from the '+' icon
- Reassign it to an Aux by right or CTRL clicking on the Track name.
- Make sure it's a stereo Aux if you have a stereo FX unit. Rename the object 'bus FX send'.

Figure 9.26

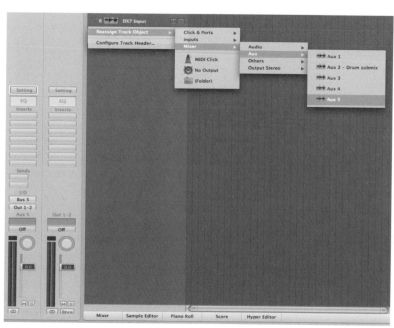

Select the outputs you have the external FX unit connected to. Say outputs 5 and 6. Set the input to No input (right).

Now, if you send to this Aux from an audio track, the Aux acts as a send to the external FX, while the live inputs are a return (below).

You can name the inputs, outputs and buses from the Mixer page's Options>I/O labels menu item.

- You can now rename the various sends, inputs and outputs.
- You can also name any input, outputs or busses on your system.

• You can also send directly to outputs and then to an external effects unit and return to inputs on a channel using the I/O plug-in. You choose the input and/or outputs from the pull down menus

Set up a MIDI Multi-Instrument object from the Environment New>Multi Instrument menu item. Connect it to the MIDI port the effects unit is connected to. You can then name and change patches on the external effects unit.

You can add Virtual effect plug-ins to Live inputs. However, there are latency issues here. See the section on Plug-in Delay Compensation (PDC) below.

If you return any external Effects or Synthesisers through Logic's input objects any latency will be compensated for by PDC.

When bouncing down a Song with External Instruments or other audio coming in through Input objects or the I/O plug-in, you must use Real Time bouncing.

Hide tracks

If you have a complex Arrange page with many Tracks, you may find yourself running out of screen 'real estate'. You can Hide tracks by clicking on the 'H' button and using the Arrange page>View>Hide Current Track and Select next Track menu item. Toggling the 'H' button on and off hides and shows the Tracks.

Side chains

Some plug-ins can be affected or controlled from another channel via their plug-in side chains. A side-chain input allows a plug-in to be controlled by another audio source. You could, for example, use a voice track to adjust a compressor on a music track causing the music to drop as the person speaks. Or you can use a complex rhythmic part to control a gate for 'chopping effects. Here, we're attempting to tighten up a

bass synthesiser part by inserting a gate on the bass track and sending a bass drum signal through a side-chain to the gate.

The drum loop is on Audio Track 1, the bass on Audio Track 2. Insert a gate on the bass track.

Select the side chain input from Track 1 (Audio 1).

Now on playback, the drum loop will control the gate.

Other uses of side chains in Logic

Autofilter. You can use a signal on the side chain of the autofilter to adjust the modulation of the filter. If you use a percussive input, the filter cutoff frequency will be modulated in time with the song.

Fuzz-wah. The side chain iinput s used to control the motion of the wah-wah filter. If you set side chain input to the same Track on which the Fuzz-Wah is instanced will produce a true auto-wah effect.

Ringshifter. When using this plug-in in Ring Modulator mode, you can use the side chain as the modulating signal, rather than its internal LFP. This produces more a more complex output.

Match EQ. This EQ uses a recording you wish to copy the EQ from and imposes the copied EQ onto a destination file. You can send the template spectrum though the side chain to Match EQ.

Plug-in delay compensation (PDC)

Tip

PDC is a playback only compensation. Logic can't anticipate the latencies involved in the recording process.

Latency, and its effect on Logic was discussed in Chapter 4. Logic has PDC to compensate for the latencies that occur when audio passes through various parts of Logic. Audio may pass through Logic in different ways. Each different path will impart different amounts of delay. One plug-in or Virtual instrument will have a different latency than another. There will also be delays when audio passes through multiple buses and Auxes. Logic uses PDC to overcome this problem.

Correctly written plug-ins will pass their latency value through to Logic and Logic will delay various parts of the recording so everything lines up.
Logic has three PDC settings. These are selected in the general section of the Audio Preferences.

- *Off.* No latency compensation occurs. Use this setting if you are using Logic in the same way you would an old-style analog Tape Recorder and taking the tracks into a mixing desk. In this case, you won't be using plug-ins. Logic will not be delayed on playback.
- *Audio tracks and instruments.* Use this setting if you are not using buses or Auxes.
- *Full.* Use this if you are using buses and Auxes and mixing totally within Logic.

Using hardware controllers in Logic

If you have a hardware controller that can send out MIDI controller data from the controls, you can use these to control various parameters in Logic. These could be anything from the Modulation, Pitch bend wheels and Expression pedals on your synthesizer to a dedicated hardware box with lots of knobs, faders and switches. Some hardware controllers have 'pre-set' assignments within Logic.

However, you can easily allow your hardware controller control of any Logic on-screen parameter manually. You could, for example, use knobs on a synthesizer that send MIDI controllers to adjust parameters on the ES-1 Virtual instrument. Choose menu item Logic Pro > Preferences > Control Surfaces > Controller Assignments

1 Click on Easy View
2 Select a parameter on the ES-1. For example, if you want to control the Filter Cutoff, just move the onscreen control on the ES-1.
3 Click Learn Mode
4 Move the physical knob or slider you want to use on your hardware controller
5 Repeat steps 3 and 4 as necessary

Automation quick access

You can quickly assign a control on a keyboard or MIDI mixer, as long as it puts out MIDI controller data when moved, to an Automation parameter. First you need to make sure that the Arrange page view>Track automation is turned ON and that the Parameter you wish to learn is chosen from the Track automation list (right).

To use automation Quick Access, open it from the Main page Options>Track Automation Settings.

Click on 'Learn Message' and slowly move your hardware control. This could be a modulation wheel, a pedal knob or a slider. Logic will tell you the Assignment has been learned. Click on 'Done'. Deselect the Learn Message button. Now, turning the knob will adjust the Automation parameter.

Panning

Each Audio, MIDI and Virtual instrument has a Pan control. You can determine how the Panning works from the Settings>Audio preferences window. There are three choices.

1 0dB – mono signals seem louder when set to the centre position and quieter at the extreme left and right pans.
2 -3dB – the level of the signal at the centre position is 3dB less than when the Pan Law is set to 0dB.
3 -3dB compensated – the level of the signal at the centre position is the same as the 0dB setting. However when the pan control is set to full left or right pan positions they will be 3dB louder than the 0dB setting.

Info

The two +/- 3dB settings attempt to maintain the output of a channel whatever value the pan control is set to.

Creating 'doubled' parts

It's often useful to record a part twice and then hard pan the first recording to the left and the second to the right. This gives the recording a fuller and wider image. This is especially useful on guitar recordings. You can simulate this effect with one recording in the following way.

• Record the part (right).

- Copy it to another Track (hold down the Option key while dragging.)

- Pan the two Regions to the left and right (pic on left).
- Select the first copy and set a delay time of +25 in the Region parameter box. Repeat with the second Region but set the delay to –25 on this one.

Info

You can improve the illusion of two recordings by using different EQ, Compression, AUPitch or even the Enhanced timing plug-in on the Tracks.

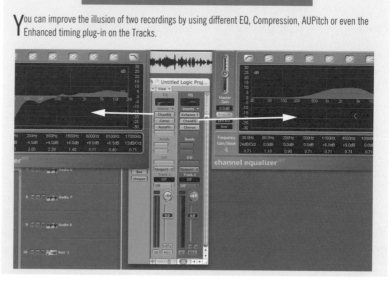

Creating harmonies from a single recording

You can use a similar technique to create harmonies.

- Record a vocal part. Copy it to another Track. Instance the AUPitch plug-in on the second Track. Change the pitch of the second Track to get the harmony you desire.

• Repeat with as many other Tracks as you require.

Automation

Logic has an extensive and fully featured automation system. Everything can be automated; levels, pans, sends, plug-in parameters, Solo and Muting. This makes it ripe for a section of automation tips and tricks.

Automation preferences

The automation preferences window can be accessed from the main Logic Preferences menu or the Options>Track Automation Settings menu.
There are several preferences available.

Move automation with Regions

This has three settings, Never, Always and Ask. Ask is probably the most useful setting as you'll almost always want to choose whether you want to move the automation data or not.

Ramp time

When you are using automation in Touch mode, this parameter defines how long it takes for an automation curve to return to the previously recorded values after you stop moving a control.

Write mode changes to: This is the mode the Track will change to after you have finished recording automation onto a Track. If you set this to Read, it will stop you accidentally overwriting any previous data.

Touch/latch/Write Erase: Here you can define which parameters can be changed when you use these automation modes. You'd normally leave all these boxes ticked.

Automation quick access: This is discussed earlier in this chapter.

Automation display preferences

There are a couple of display-based preferences that relate to automation. They are in the Display preference's Arrange section.

You can define the transparency of the Regions (objects) and the associated automation data (other). This can make it easier to see the automation on a Track. To see this effect, you need to have a high zoom setting.

You can edit any automation data on a Track in the Event List editor by using the Automation Event Edit Key Command.

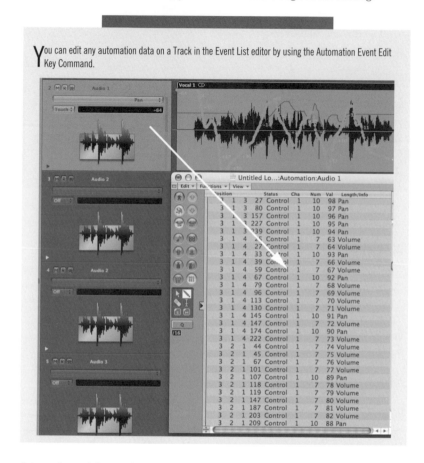

Automation and the vocal track – using the mouse for automation

Automation has revolutionised the mixing process. You can fine-tune volume and other parameters to such an extent that you can easily eliminate or suppress faults in the recording process – or with the person being recorded. Vocals usually the most prominent feature in a song so it's vitally important it sounds right. We all know what a voice should sound like – we all have one! The following tips are all about creating the perfect vocal track.

The first place to start is by removing any excessive breaths and other extraneous noises in between the actual singing lines using the mouse. The following figure is a typical vocal recording split it into individual phrases and compiled of various takes.

First, you need to make sure track automation is visible by using the Arrange page View, Track automation menu item. Now, select 'Volume' from the Automation data pull down menu. Also make sure the Automation mode is set to 'Read'.

You'll see the volume automation line appear. The easiest way to draw automation curves around these vocal phrases is to drag a box around them while holding down the Shift, Ctrl and Option keys simultaneously. On releasing the mouse, four automation nodes will be created. Repeat this for all the vocal phrases.

If you drag the line in-between phrases down, you'll see volume curves created around each phrase.

Now you can use the mouse to edit this data. If you zoom the track or the window you can see the curves in more detail. Nodes can be dragged around using the mouse. You can also use 'S' shaped curves (chosen from the drop down menu under the Toolbox. Once you have volume automation curves around each phrase you can do some finer editing.

Info

In Logic Pro 9 you can add four automation nodes to the boundaries of a Region using the Key commands Create 2 or 4 nodes at Region boundaries. If you split a vocal take into Regions using the Arrange page's Audio>Strip silence menu item, you can easily create nodes around the separate phrases.

Removing or lowering breath noises

You can change the feel of a vocal recording by lowering or completely removing the vocalist's breathing – especially noticeable if you're using a compressor plug-in on the voice. Breaths at the start of phrases are dealt with by the method described above – just move the start curve of the automation 'islands' until the breath is cut out. If you have a breath within a phrase, you'll probably want to work in a slightly different way.

• Drag a box around the breath noise while holding down the Shift, Ctrl and Option keys simultaneously to create 4 nodes.

- Now drag down the line between the nodes. You'll probably find that removing the breath within a phrase completely will sound unnatural, so you may just want to reduce the level a little.

- You can now drag nodes around to fine-tune where the volume drop goes.

Reducing the effects of plosives and sibilance

These are the bane of vocal recordings. You can always use a hardware or software de-esser to try and remove sibilance, but these can often sound unnatural. With total automation available, you can deal with each case by reducing the volume for a small period of time at the point of the offending sibilance or plosive. Listen through to the vocal track in solo mode and at a high on-screen zoom magnification. When you reach a sibilant 'S' or a popping 'P', stop the sequencer. Create three nodes by clicking just before and after the area and one inside these two nodes. Drag down the middle node (left).

You need to listen to the automation to make sure you haven't gone too far. You'll probably need to finely edit the start end and drop of the automation too. S-shaped curves are also useful in this situation, as they seem to help in getting a more naturalistic effect.

The drop in volume only needs to be of the order of milliseconds to reduce the effect of sibilance or pops – any more and you'll hear definite volume drops. Using this method on sibilance keeps the track sounding bright and doesn't produce that 'toothless' effect that de-essers can sometimes cause. It's hard work but rewarding. Of course, you may have to modify this automation further later in the mix process – automation can rarely be done in isolation.

You can use this technique for any track that needs fine volume editing - and not just volume. If you look at the Track automation list automation pull-down menu (left) you'll see the automatable parameters of all the plug-ins on a track along with volume, pan, solo, mute, any sends and effects bypass. This latter one is particularly useful if you want a plug-in to only affect part of a track. You can add echo just to the end of vocal phrases by un-bypassing an effect at a particular point in the track. Some plug-ins can cause pops when you do this. If this is the case, insert the plug-in on a bus and automate the send to that bus instead (Figure 9.64).

It's easy to see how powerful this technique is. Another thing to try are to adjust the output, ratio and threshold of a compressor during a song to help the vocal sit in the mix. It's also easy to increase sends to delays or reverbs when a mix gets busy and reduce the levels for a drier sound during sparser sections.

Figure 9.64

While it may seem more natural to use Logic's automation system with a hardware controller or on-screen knobs, the mouse-based editing features are essential for fine-tuning and so shouldn't be overlooked.

Stem mixing

One of the annoying limitations of Logic's automation system is that there is no way to increase or reduce all the automation data in one go. Consider a typical mixing scenario you've adjusted all your backing tracks until you're happy with the mix, but you need a few extra dB on vocals and bass drum. However, just raising the levels of these tracks takes the master over 0dB. What you really want to do is lower all the other tracks proportionally instead. To do this, you'll have to lower the volume *and, perhaps, other automation data* on each track! Imagine how long this would take if you have 48 tracks with complex and multiple automation data! The section 'Editing automation data with the mouse', below, lists various mouse-based commands that can help to make this easier, but you may also want to think of mixing using the 'stem' technique.

What this means in practice is sending several similar tracks to busses. You could, for example, send all the drums to one bus, backing vocals to another, guitars to another and so on. Balancing would then be just a matter of adjusting the level of these busses rather than overall tracks –and you can automate these busses too. Individual 'stems' can be compressed individually – which also helps in getting things to 'sit in the mix'. Of course, you will still have to edit other automation data, such as a synthesisers' filter cut-off individually for each track – but you're unlikely to want to do this simultaneously on many instruments.

Editing automation data with the mouse

The way nodes and lines are created and edited in Logic are affected with modifier keys. Here's a handy list of these.

Creating automation nodes with the Arrow Tool

- Add a new node by a short click anywhere on the Track.
- Add a new node on an existing line with a short click on the automation line.
- To create 4 nodes around a part of a region hold down the Shift, Ctrl and Alt keys and rubberband the area you wish to create nodes over. See the main body for information about a bug with this under Logic 7.1.
- To create 2 nodes around a part of a region hold down the Shift and Alt keys and rubberband the area you wish to create nodes over.

Selecting Automation data with the Arrow tool

- Select a node by clicking and holding on node. A little info window will appear giving you details about the node.
- Select a line by clicking and holding on the line.

Selecting a group of nodes

- Hold down the Shift key and rubberband around the nodes. You must do this within the boundary of a region; otherwise you'll select the region itself. You can then move the whole selection by dragging the lines or the nodes within the selection.
- To select all Automation from nearest node to the song's end, Hold down the Alt key and click on the node.
- To select all Automation on a track, hold down the Alt key and DOUBLE click on a node.
- Selecting automation nodes with the Automation Tool set to 'Select'.
- To select ALL the automation on a region just click on the region.
- To select non-continuous areas and extend areas, hold down the Shift key and rubberband each area.

De-selecting automation nodes

To de-select ALL automation, click outside the track.

Moving automation

- To move single nodes just click and drag a node.
- To move single automation lines, just click and drag the line.
- To move a selection of nodes horizontally (forwards/backwards in time), click-hold and drag a line or node.
- To move a selection of nodes vertically (increment or decrement), click-hold and drag a line or node.
- Moving automation with the Automation tool set to 'curve'.
- In this mode, dragging a line will result in a curve. Depending on where you drag the line, the curve will be either a 'smile' shape or 'S' shaped. You can do this with the Arrow tool while holding down the Alt and Control keys and a long click on the line.

Scaling automation data

To scale selected automation data up and down (increment or decrement) proportionally, click-hold and drag NOT on a Line or Node. To do this to a whole tracks' visible data, hold down the Command key and drag the level slider to the right of the Instrument column up or down.

Copying automation data

To copy a selection of automation data with the Arrow Tool, hold down the Alt key, and click-hold and drag the selection.

Deleting automation data

- Delete a node with a short click on the node.

- To delete selected Automation data use the backspace key (but check no objects are selected as well!)
- To delete all Automation data of track hold down the Shift and Alt keys and double click on the track.

Inserting a reverb or delay plug-in on a bus – the wet/dry setting

When you use a Tracks Send control to route audio to a bus with a reverb or delay plug-in inserted, you are effectively bleeding off a little of the audio passing through that Track and mixing the effected signal in with the dry signal passing through the Track (right).

In these cases you should set the 'Dry' or 'Direct' signal to zero and the 'Reverb' or 'Wet' or Mix control to its fullest extent (below).

Pre and post sends

You can choose between these modes on a Track object's Send controls.

Post. The Send knob is connected to the Channel strip's volume control. This means that when you reduce the level on the Track, the send level reduces at the same level thus maintaining the relative level of the effect.

Pre. In this case, when you reduce the volume fader the effect on the bus remains the same. It's really useful as an effect or for setting up monitor mixes where you can send signals to monitors without the main volumes being up.

Pre fader metering

When this is ON, the level of the Track is still displayed even if the volume slider is on zero.

MIDI mixing tips

External MIDI equipment

Consider recording external synthesizer sounds that are being played back by Logic's MIDI sequencer. You can do this in two ways

- Route the synthesizer into Logic via a recording Track and record as you would a microphone or guitar.
- Route the synthesizer into Logic using an Input track, solo the track and bounce it down. In real time

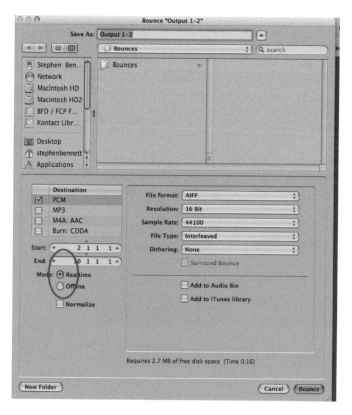

- Re-import the bounce file and drag it from the Audio window to line up with the original MIDI data.

MIDI compression

The Dynamics parameter in the Region Parameter box in the Inspector is a sort of 'compressor' for MIDI data (right). Hold the mouse key down to change the values from a pop up menu. This parameter changes the differences between the softest and loudest velocity values in a Region. Values over 100% expand the dynamic range of the values, increasing the difference between the softest and loudest velocity values, while those less than 100% decrease the difference, or compress, the values.

Some mixing tips using Logic's plug-ins

Processing drums

Individual drums may require different effects. In addition the whole kit, or sections of the kit can also be processed with the same effects.

Processing the bass drum

EQ: Try cutting or boosting the frequency at about 300Hz by about 10dB. This should clear up any muddiness in the sound. You may also want to boost the high frequencies at around 5000 to 6000Hz if the drum sounds really dull. Boosting the frequency at around 40 to 100Hz, perhaps as a shelf EQ, will add weight to the sound.

Compression: The bass drum is often the main pulse of a song, so it's important that its level is even. If you are finding that the level varies a lot, try the following settings on a compressor.

Ratio For a mild compression effect set the ratio at 4:1. For a more aggressive effect set it to 10:1

Attack: Set this to 1 to 5 ms or fast. This means the signal is affected quickly – i.e. the compressor works right away to keep sound level in volume. This is particularly important with percussive sounds.

Release: Set this to around 0.2s. You'll need to experiment with this value. If the sound starts to 'pump', or jump rapidly up and down in level, reduce the value.

Threshold: Turn down the threshold control until the compressor starts to work (you'll see the gain reduction in the meter on the compressor). Further reduce the control until you get a nice level sound.

Tip

Keep bypassing the EQ and compressor to see what effect they are having on the sound and to set the processed level to the same as the unprocessed one.

Gain make up: Increase the value of the gain make up control until the bass drum is at the same level as the non-compressed sound.

Gate: You can isolate each bass drum hit by gating the individual hits. You'll have to do this by ear. Solo the bass drum and adjust the threshold and attack and release controls of the gate until you only hear the bass drum.

Pan: Pan the bass drum to the centre (right).

Tip

You may want to keep de-soloing the individual drums so you can hear them in context as you process.

Processing the snare drum

EQ: Try boosting the frequency at about 5000Hz to 6000Hz to add a bit of brightness to the sound. You can 'thicken' up the snare by boosting a few dB at around 60Hz to 100Hz. If the snare sounds muddy try a cut at around 300Hz. If the snare sounds too harsh, try cutting a few dB at 1000Hz.

Compression

Try these settings as a starting point.

Ratio: for a mild compression effect set the ratio at 4:1. For a more aggressive effect set it to 10:1

Attack: Set this to 1 to 5 ms or fast. This means the signal is affected quickly – i.e. the compressor works right away to keep sound level in volume.

Release: Set this to around 0.2s. You'll need to experiment with this value. If the sound starts to 'pump' reduce the value.

Threshold: Turn down the threshold control until the compressor starts to work (you'll see the gain reduction in the meter on the compressor). Further reduce the control until you get a nice level sound.

Gain make up: Increase the value of the gain make up control until the snare drum is at the same level as the non-compressed sound.

Gate: You can isolate each snare drum hit by gating the individual hits in the same ways as the bass drum.

Pan: Pan the snare to the same position it was when recording. Usually the snare sits slightly to the left of the drummer from their perspective. So to hear it from a listener's point of view, pan it slightly to the right.

Overhead microphones

You'll treat the two overhead tracks in exactly the same way – as a stereo recording.

EQ: Try boosting the overheads at around 10000Hz to add brightness – try using a slope filter. You may also want to roll off the low end to reduce the effect of the bass and/or snare drums in the overheads.

Compression: At this stage, just add a gentle compression to the overheads.

Ratio: For a mild compression effect set the ratio at 2:1 or 4:1

Attack: Set this to 1 to 5 ms or fast. This means the signal is affected quickly – i.e. the compressor works right away to keep sound level in volume.

Release: Set this to around 0.2s. You'll need to experiment with this value. If the sound starts to 'pump' reduce the value.

Threshold: Turn down the threshold control until the compressor starts to work (you'll see the gain reduction in the meter on the compressor). Further reduce the control until you get a nice level sound.

Gain make up: Increase the value of the gain make up control until the overheads are at the same level as the non-compressed sound.

Pan: Pan the overhead tracks hard left and right. Remember; the listener will hear the opposite panning that the drummer hears, so pan the left overhead hard right and vice-versa (see pic on right).

Processing an Aux drum mix

We'll use a bus to process the whole drum mix. This Aux will allow us to adjust the level of the whole kit using one fader.

Create or select an Aux. Make sure it is a stereo Aux. Make sure the outputs of the individual drum tracks run through the Aux rather than going straight to the Master outputs (right). Now the fader, solo and mute buttons on the Aux will affect the all four of the drum tracks at the same time.

Compressing the whole drum track

A lot of modern music uses heavily compressed drums. How much you use on a whole drum sub-mix depends on the type of track you are producing.

Insert a compressor on the bus (Figure 9.78). Try these settings as a starting point:

Ratio: For a mild compression effect set the ratio at 4:1. For a more aggressive effect set it to 10:1

Attack: Set this to 1 to 5 ms or fast. This means the signal is affected quickly – i.e. the compressor works right away to keep sound level in volume.

Figure 9.78

Release: Set this to around 0.2s. You'll need to experiment with this value. If the sound starts to 'pump' reduce the value – unless this is the effect you want!

Threshold: Turn down the threshold control until the compressor starts to work (you'll see the gain reduction in the meter on the compressor). Further reduce the control until you get a nice level sound. If you want a heavily compressed sound, pull the fader down more.

Gain make up: Increase the value of the gain make up control until the drum sub-mix is at the same level as the non-compressed sound.

Processing guitars

Electric guitars

EQ: Try boosting the frequency around 3000Hz to 6000Hz to brighten up a dull sound. Try cutting the same frequencies if you have a harsh sound. If the guitar sounds indistinct, try cutting the frequencies at 300Hz.

Compression: Electric guitars are often heavily compressed when recording. Depending on the type of music you are recording you may want to compress them some more. Try these settings as a starting point.

Ratio: Try a compression ratio in the range 8:1 to 10:1

Attack: Set this to 2 to 5 ms or fast. This means the signal is affected quickly – i.e. the compressor works right away to keep sound level in volume.

Release: Set this to around 0.5s. You'll need to experiment with this value.

Threshold: Turn down the threshold control until the compressor starts to work (you'll see the gain reduction in the meter on the compressor). Further reduce the control until you get a nice level sound.

Gain make up: Increase the value of the gain make up control until the guitar is at the same level as the non-compressed sound.

Pan: Panning guitars is an artistic decision. If you have two guitars or a guitar and a keyboard you may want to pan each slightly left and right.

Acoustic guitars

You can try the same EQ and compression settings on acoustic guitar as on the electric guitar. However, in general, you'll probably use less compression and a little frequency boost at around 2000Hz to 3000Hz to accentuate the plucked sound.

Processing bass

EQ: For a deep, bassy sound try boosting a little around 40Hz. To reduce muddiness cut a little at 300Hz. You can even try adding boosting at 2000Hz to accentuate the 'twang'.

Compression

Try these settings as a starting point.

Ratio: Try a compression ratio in the range 4:1 to 10:1

Attack: Set this to 2 to 10 ms. A longer time produces a more 'compressed' sound. Very short attack can give the bass a distorted 'growl'.

Release: Set this to around 0.5s. You'll need to experiment with this value. Often it's nice on bass to leave the compressor 'open', using a long release, to give the bass more sustain.

Threshold: Turn down the threshold control until the compressor starts to work (you'll see the gain reduction in the meter on the compressor). Further reduce the control until you get a nice level sound.

Gain make up: Increase the value of the gain make up control until the bass is at the same level as the non-compressed sound.

Pan: Bass is usually panned in the centre along with the bass drum.

Keyboards

Keyboard instruments often have a wide frequency range that can interfere with other instruments and recordings. You may want to try cutting the low, mid and high frequencies, depending on the song. You can also boost the very highs for an 'airy' effect.

Keyboards are often in stereo so you can pan to any suitable point.

Some panning ideas

Panning places the sound in a position in the stereo field. You can use panning to position different elements of a mix in different position to increase clarity. In theory, you can pan any instrument anywhere. However, low frequency instruments such as bass drum or bass are usually panned to the centre, as are vocals. Judicious use of panning can help simulate the effect of a group of instruments spread out over the stereo field. You can also use panning as an effect – swinging the sound from one speaker to another.

Processing vocals

If your song has vocals, they will usually be the most important part of the arrangement. A poor vocal is the often main reason a recording can sound 'non professional'. Vocalists vary tremendously, as do the microphones used to record them. As vocals are the one instrument we all possess and can use to a greater or lesser extent, we are very sensitive to problems with recordings of the voice.

As well as the lead voice you may also have backing vocals, which are usually processed in a slightly different way to enhance their differences.

Processing backing vocals

Depending on what type of backing vocals you have, it may be a good idea to separate them in frequency from the lead vocal in the mix. On each separate backing vocal track you can try.

EQ: Try boosting the upper frequencies, say at 10000Hz to make the vocal more airy. You may also want to reduce the low frequency content to accentuate this effect. If the vocals sound nasal, reduce the frequencies at 3000Hz to 4000Hz. Use a shelf filter to cut out low frequencies and traffic rumble noise.

Pan the backing vocals. Where you pan them depends on how many backing vocals you have recorded.

Send the backing vocals to a bus in the same way as you did with the drum mix (pic right). Now compress the backing vocal sub mix by inserting a compressor on the bus (Figure 9.84).

Figure 9.84

Try these settings as a starting point.

Ratio: 4:1 to 10:1

Attack: Set this to 2 to 5 ms or fast. This means the signal is affected quickly – i.e. the compressor works right away to keep sound level in volume.

Release: Set this to around 0.3s. You'll need to experiment with this value.

Threshold: Turn down the threshold control until the compressor starts to work (you'll see the gain reduction in the meter on the compressor). Further reduce the control until you get a nice level sound. If you want a heavily compressed sound, pull the fader down more.

Gain make up: Increase the value of the gain make up control until the backing vocals are at the same level as the non-compressed sound.

Processing lead vocals

EQ: Try boosting a small amount at 5000Hz to 60000Hz. Be careful with increasing the high frequencies on vocals; this can lead to sibilance, especially on 's' words. Boosting the upper frequencies at about 10000Hz will make the vocal more airy. If the vocals sound nasal, reduce the frequencies at 3000Hz to 4000Hz. You may need to reduce the frequencies at around 300Hz to increase clarity. Use a shelf filter to cut out low frequency and rumble noise.

Compression

You can use a lot of different types of compression on vocals. If you have a vocalist with a wide dynamic range, you'll have to compress more to get the vocal to 'sit' in the mix. It's common to use a 'classic' compressor plug-in on vocals to enhance the sound further. Try this range of settings as a starting point.

Ratio 2:1 to 10:1

Attack: Set this to 2 to 5 ms or fast. This means the signal is affected quickly – i.e. the compressor works right away to keep sound level in volume.

Release: Set this to around 0.3s to 0.5s. You'll need to experiment with this value.

Threshold: Turn down the threshold control until the compressor starts to work (you'll see the gain reduction in the meter on the compressor). Further reduce the control until you get a nice level sound. If you want a heavily compressed sound, pull the fader down more.

Gain make up: Increase the value of the gain make up control until the vocals are at the same level as the non-compressed sound.

Frequency in Hz

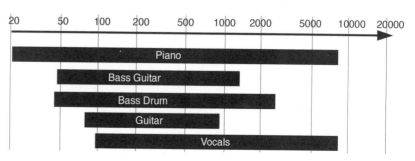

Automation level adjustment versus compression

Using compression to maintain a constant level has a very specific effect that may or may not be suitable for a given occasion. Using automation produces a more 'natural' sound.

Making a vocal 'sit' in the mix

Vocal recordings which have no ambience can sound dull or dry. Many vocal recordings use reverb or delay to help make them sound more natural. If you use too long a reverb or delay time however, the vocal may sound drowned out and indistinct. As a rule of thumb, you can use a longer reverb or delay on slower tracks, with less on faster or more intimate ones. Long reverb or delay times will make the vocal sound distant, so it's logical that using short delays or reverbs will make them seem closer and more intimate.

To add reverb to a vocal track:
- Create a stereo bus. Insert a reverb plug-in on the bus.

Figure 9.86

- Select a suitable reverb.
- Set the wet/dry control to 100% wet (reverb). We want none of the 'dry' sound to pass through the bus. Leave the bus level at 0 dB.
- On the track mixer strip, use the send control to direct some of the signal to the bus (right).
- Adjust the level of the send so that it enhances the vocal sound. You may also want to try adjusting the pre-delay, the reverb time and high frequency filters to make the reverb duller sounding compared to the unprocessed vocals. Too bright a reverb can cause excessive sibilance.

Now play back the track. Bring up send control to the bus until you can just hear the reverb, then pull down the level of the send a little.

Adding delay to a vocal track

Set up the bus as described for the reverb, but insert a stereo delay plug-in instead.

Creating a 'dry, but full of presence' vocal sound

Modern vocals seem to be very 'dry' in the mix. But you'll find that if you use no reverb or delay with the vocal at all it sounds more 'dead and boxy' than dry and present. The way to get the 'Dry, but full of presence' sound is either with a very short reverb or by using a stereo delay.

- Set the left delay time to around 350ms, the right to 300ms.
- Set the feedback to around 50% for each channel.
- If the delay has built in EQ, cut the high frequencies over 2500 Hz.

Now play back the track. Bring up send control to the bus until you can just hear the delay then pull down the level of the send a little. The vocal should still sound 'dry' but have presence.

Using send effects on other tracks

Whenever we want to blend a little of an effect with a 'dry' track, rather then putting the whole track through an effect (insert effect), we need to use a send effect. In this case a plug-in effect is placed on a bus and the amount of the effect audible is determined by the send control.

In general you'll use reverb and delay as send effects, EQ, compressions and modulation as insert effects – but that's not a cut and dried rule.

Info

Send effects also have an added advantage in terms of system performance. You can send several different tracks to a single bus. You could, for example, send the snare drum, guitar and keyboards to a single bus with a reverb inserted on it. This can be useful if you're trying to produce a track that sounds like it was recorded in the same acoustic 'space'. It also means you use less CPU power – you only need one reverb to process many different tracks.

Mastering

Introduction

Mastering used to mean the process of preparing a tape recording for cutting onto vinyl. Mastering engineers with years of experience would prepare the tape with specialised EQ to fit the recording onto the disc. With the advent of CD and digital recording, Mastering has come to mean something quite different. Mastering may involve any or all of the following processes:

- Arranging each song in the correct order (Compiling).
- Level matching each song so that there are no jumps in volume between them.
- Fade in and fade out the songs, or use crossfades if you want the songs to blend into each other.
- Processing with broad range EQ, Compression and Limiting to add a professional 'sheen' to the recordings and to make them sound cohesive when listened to as a whole.
- Creating a Master CD-R from which you can produce normal audio CDs or further CD-Rs.

Mastering is often said to be the process whereby you can add the professional 'gloss' to a recording. It's usually seen as a kind of arcane art. However, Audio recording software offers us the tools to produce our own masters, using the same tools we used for recording and mixing. As with mixing, listening to your own CD collections is a good way to hear what a good mastered recording sounds like and to compare it with your own work.

You will often hear people say that you cannot do your own mastering – you really need to send your mixes to a specialist. While it is true that there are many talented people with esoteric equipment available at high cost, it is very possible for you to master your songs yourself. Mastering isn't magic; it's like any process of recording. You need to practice, experiment, listen and try and fail before you get a good 'ear'.

You may want to master each song separately and then arrange them into the correct order afterwards. This may also be a useful method if you are using plug-ins that require a lot of CPU power.

Most of the tools you'll need are exactly the same as the ones you have used when recording and mixing. A large part of the mastering process will entail the use of these plug-ins.

Arranging the songs into the correct order.

Let's say, for example, you have 10 songs to compile. Create 10 audio tracks in your audio hardware. Make sure they are stereo. Load in each song file to each track. Drag them to the order you require.

The type of mastering processing required will depend on the songs themselves. Even if you have recorded and mixed all the songs is the same way you'll find that they vary quite a bit in volume and tone.

Adjusting the level

You can use your Logic's s automation to level match the tracks. If you listen to a few minutes of the end on one track through to the first few minutes of the next, you'll get an idea of the relative volume levels of the tracks. You can then adjust the track levels using volume automation.

If you want track fade-ins and fade-outs you can use volume automation for this as well.

Crossfading from one track to another is also possible using volume automation.

Next, we'll want to process the songs with plug-ins. You don't always have to do this; processing isn't always needed. You may find that the mix sounds exactly the way you want it to as it is. In this case you can skip the processing section and jump right through to the 'Bouncing down the master' section.

However, most mixes will benefit from processing. You don't necessarily need to use all these plug-ins on every track. You'll need to make some creative decisions when listening to your songs.
There are two ways to master several songs for a complete CD

Processing each song individually
Each song will need to have the following processors inserted onto each individual track. Note that this method uses a lot of CPU power, as you will, in this example, need to have 10 of each of the plug-ins running at the same time.

Compression
You may want to use compression to 'level' out a completed and mixed song. Many compressors have a 'sound', which they will impose on the songs. Some compression plug-ins simulate valve or classic compressors, which again have their own specific 'sound'.

The problems with compressing a whole track is that one element of the sound, say the bass drum, may trigger the compressor in a way that isn't suitable for the rest of the track. You may find the track 'pumping' or distorting in some way. Gentle compression is usually needed here.

Try these settings as a starting point
Ratio: try a compression ratio in the range 2:1 to 5:1
Attack: set this to 2ms or fast. This means the signal is affected quickly – i.e. the compressor works right away to keep sound level in volume.
Release: set this to around 0.5s. You'll need to experiment with this value. To slow a release will make the sound unnatural.
Threshold: turn down the threshold control until the compressor starts to work (you'll see the gain reduction in the meter on the compressor). Further reduce the control until you get a nice level sound.
Gain make up: increases the value of the gain make-up control until the compressed song is at the same level as the non-compressed one.

Multi band compression
One way to get around the problems with 'normal' compression is to use a multi band compressor. These split the audio stream into many frequency bands – usually 3 or 4. The frequency ranges of the bands are variable and each band has its own compressor. The idea behind multi band compressors is that you can affect various frequency ranges in different ways. For example, you could compress the mid range more than the bass, or select a narrow frequency range to correct for excessive sibilance.

Some multi band compressors allow individual threshold levels to be adjusted along with an 'overall' one. You can 'solo' each individual frequency band to hear the effect on that band alone.

Tip

Whether you process using the EQ first or the compression first is a debatable point. You can experiment with both ways and see which works best for you.

Tip

Remember to keep bypassing the plug-in(s) to hear the effect they are having on the songs. Processing, especially boosting frequencies using EQ, will often increase the overall volume. This increase in volume can easily be mistaken as a 'better' sound. Try to keep the processed and bypassed sound at the same level.

Multi band compressors are complex beastS by their very nature and the parameters available may vary. However they usually come with a range of presets to get you started.

EQ (Equalisation or tone correction)

Whereas during mixing we were often using EQ to correct and enhance individual instruments, when mastering it's a more gentle correction that is required. You may want to subtly enhance the high frequencies or reduce or enhance the bass.

The EQ you use is going to be dependent on the type of song you are mastering and the result you are trying to get – but here are a few settings to try as a starting point.

- Boost a few dBs at around 15000Hz to add 'air' to the track – but watch for sibilance.
- Boost at around 80Hz to enhance the low end. Cut at 300Hz to remove muddiness. Don't be tempted to use too much boost or cut.

Limiting or Maximising

Limiting is the last effect you should use in the mastering chain. It's a severe form of compression, which stops the output going over a certain pre-set level. This will allow you to push the level as high as possible without hitting

Info

See Chapter 5 for more on Logic's Multiband compressors.

Tip

You can use the Multi Meter to display the overall frequency range for a song. This can be extremely useful to see if you have any gross 'bumps' in the frequency range of your song. However, it always best to confirm any analysis by using your ears!

Tip

You may want to use a third-party 'classic' emulation of EQ and/or compression to enhance the overall 'tone' of the mix.

Tip

If you find that you are boosting or cutting frequencies by a large amount to make the song sound OK, you should consider re-mixing the song.

0dB and digital distortion. In addition, limiters often have the facility to pull up low-level signals, thus compressing the sound into a narrow volume range. These limiters are often called maximisers.

The Ad Limiter is most suitable for mastering. Insert it after the EQ and Compressor and try the following settings as a guide:

- Set the Out ceiling to –0.3 dB. This will stop the level ever going higher than this.
- Set the Input Scale to 0dB.
- Set the Gain to 0dB.
- Play the Track.
- Initially bring up the Gain control to increase apparent loudness. You may have to reduce the gain and increase the Input to get a musically useful result (right).

Processing all the songs with the same plug-ins and settings

You'll can exactly the same plug-ins when processing each channel separately, but you'll put them on the master stereo output instead of each individual track. This means that all the songs will be processed by the same plug-in parameters.

You can of course, use a combination of the two techniques. For example you could have individual EQ and/or compression on each track, but the limiter on the master output only.

Other mastering effects

While the above are the 'classic' mastering effects, you may also like to try some other plug-ins to enhance your songs.

Logic's Exciter

This is a specialised plug-in that applies EQ, distortion and compression to make the sound more 'present' and brighter in tone. Exciters can initially make things sound very impressive – but may be wearing on the ear after a while, so be careful how you apply them.

Valve emulators

These plug-ins add a 'warmth' to the sound. Overused, they can make things sound woolly and muddy.

Bouncing down the mix

This is done in exactly the same way as for mixing – except that you need to use 16 bit 44.1kHz as the file format if you are transferring to CD. However, as you'll usually be be converting from a higher bit rate and/or sample rate you'll need to 'dither' the audio when you bounce down. Dither is a specialised filtering technique that smoothes out the data and reduces artifacts from the conversion. Logic uses the POW-r dithering algorithm.

Info

There is a current trend to use limiting to obtain the loudest volume and song energy as possible. While this type of mastering may sound OK on an FM radio or iPod, it does usually produce audible artifacts and can be harsh and tiring to listen to.

Info

Use Logic Pro's Export>All tracks as audio files to create individual audio files for each song.

Info

Logic Pro 9 also has Apogee's UV22HR dithering plug-in. The same selection criteria apply as for the POW-r ones.

POW-r dithering algorithm

Logic's internal resolution is 32 bit floating point. However, you will often bounce down to 24 bit for mastering or 16 bit files for CD creation. Dithering reduces unwanted graininess and quantisation noise produced during this bit reduction. The POW-r algorithm has three types of dithering. Which one you use depends on the source file. As usual, let your ears be the judge. However, some use examples are given below.

None: No dithering occurs. Use this if you want to re-import audio for mastering or adding to an already recorded track.

POW-r #1: Uses a dithering curve to reduce noise. Use on acoustic music that has been recorded at a decent level or natural sounding music.

POW-r #2: Uses noise shaping to add an extra 10dB to the dynamic range. Use on low level recorded acoustic or anywhere you need the added dynamic range.

POW-r #3: Uses noise shaping to extend the dynamic range by 20dB in the 2 to 4 kHz range. This is the range most sensitive to the human ear. Use on pop, rock or dance music or music destined for the radio. Or voice recordings.

Tip

Dithering should only be performed on the final bounce of before final CD production. If you try to dither already dithered audio, sound quality will suffer.

Order of mastering plug-ins

There are some rules about the ordering of the plug-ins on a channel strip for mastering, and some areas of flexibility.

EQ and compression

Which goes first is a matter of taste. If you use the routing method shown on the right, the EQ cannot compensate for any dulling of the sound caused by the compressor. Also, the EQ frequencies that have been boosted will get compressed more than those that have not.

Of course you could have the second routing. Which may solve that problem!

If you use the third routing, you'll get a different sound, as the EQ won't be affected by peaks in the audio.

So, here's a suggested order for your mastering plug-ins.

1 EQ or Compression (single or multiband)
2 Compression or EQ (single or multiband)
3 Exciter or valve emulator (if needed)
4 Limiter or Maximiser
5 Dither (if needed)

Appendix 1
Glossary

Analogue to digital converter (ADC)
Converts analogue signals (guitars, drums, vocals) into digital signal (bits) that a computer can read.

AES/EBU
A digital input/output, usually on XLR sockets.

Amplitude
The 'loudness' of an audio signal.

Analog(ue)
With respect to audio signals, analogue refers to a continuous waveform, as opposed to a digital one that is described a series of steps. Americans use the term analog.

ADC
Analogue to digital converter. The opposite of a DAC.

ASIO
Audio stream input output. A generic system for handling audio input and output on audio interfaces.

Audio interface
This is the hardware that allows audio to be input and output from your computer. It could be as simple as the stereo in/out card or built in soundcard or as complex as a multi in and out system with extra DSP processing.

Bank select
A combination of MIDI controller numbers 0 and 32. This command allows you to change the banks in a MIDI device and was introduced to overcome the limitation of 128 patch change numbers accessible via MIDI.

Bit
The smallest unit of digital information described as a '1' or a 0'.

Byte
An 8 bit binary number. A kilobyte is 1024 bytes, a megabyte is 1024 kilobytes and so on.

Buffer
A portion of computer memory that stores information before it is read to and from a hard disk. A buffer basically speeds up hard disk recording.

CD ripper
A program which allows the direct transfer of data from an audio CD to a hard disk audio file.

Clipping
Clipping occurs when audio levels exceed 0dB or 90 withing Logic Pro. This is a bad thing. You should not exceed these levels unless you deliberately want to make your audience's ears bleed.

Control change
MIDI control changes are used to control a wide variety of functions on a MIDI device. Some are universal such as:
Different manufacturers use other controller values for different applications. For example a MIDI controlled mixer may use MIDI controllers to adjust its values, or a MIDI effects unit may use MIDI controllers to adjust the various parameters. The upshot of this is that using a MIDI sequencer like Logic Pro you can set up 'virtual interfaces' for MIDI devices and record the changes into the sequencer.

Core Audio
All audio software under OSX uses the Core Audio drivers built into the operating system. This means that a single audio interface only needs one driver (the core audio one) to be available for all installed software such as Logic Pro and iTunes.

Core MIDI

All MIDI software under OSX uses the Core MIDI drivers built into the operating system. This means that a single MIDI interface only needs one driver (the core midi one) for it to be available for all installed software such as Logic Pro and iTunes.

CPU

The 'brain' or Central Processing Unit of a computer.

Cut, copy and paste

You may be familiar with these terms for cutting out or copying a portion of a sequence and pasting it into a new position. Logic Pro, confusingly, uses the terms 'Snip, splice and insert' to perform the same functions.

Cycle

The process of cycling or looping around a predefined section of a song.

DAC

Digital to audio converter. Converts digital data to analogue data.

DAT

Digital audio tape. A 16 bit digital tape recorder that records at sample rates of 44.1Khz and 48kHz.

Decibel (dB)

dBs are used to describe the loudness of audio signals on a logarithmic scale.

Defragment

When a hard disk fills up with files, the data that the files contain become spread across the whole disk, filling up the spaces between data. This non-contiguous file storage slows down hard disk access. Defragmenting often will speed up hard disk access – very important when recording Audio.

Digital

With respect to audio, digital signals are made up of discrete steps representing analogue waveforms. For example if you sample an analogue waveform at 44.1kHz you will have 44100 steps every second. The amplitude of the waveform is described by the number of bits. CD is 16bit, 44.1kHz digital recording. In general the more bits and the higher the sample rate, the more accurately the digital representation of the analogue waveform.

Driver

Software providing communication between a piece of hardware (audio interface, display) and the computer operating system. OSX uses a Core Audio driver.

Dongle

A hardware key allowing Logic Pro to run. Alternatively, a source of immense annoyance when it breaks down, doesn't work, or you leave it behind when you take Logic Pro out of your studio!

Drop in

Like Punch in. An automatic way of putting Logic Pro into record at a predefined point in the song.

DSP

Digital signal processing. Term used for any audio feature that uses the computer to emulate hardware units such as synthesisers, effects units and so on. DSP can be done either using the computer's main processor or additional external DSP chips, depending on which audio interface you have.

Editor

A window within a sequencer where you can edit MIDI data.

Environment

In Logic Pro, the Environment is the window where you will define your MIDI devices, patch in MIDI modifiers and set up virtual mixing desks and editors.

EQ

Equalisation. Tone manipulation. EQ can vary from simple bass and treble controls to sophisticated multi-band parametric EQ.

Event

In Logic Pro, an event is MIDI data. It can be note data, controller data, SysEx data or meta events and so on.

Fixing

Making edits in MIDI events, such as volume changes and quantization permanent. Also known in Logic Pro-speak as Normalization.

Flex Time

Logic Pro's version of fluid audio allowing the user to treat audio data as if it were MIDI with respect to timing.

Folder

A folder in Logic Pro is analogous to a folder or directory on a computer. A folder can contain other sequences.

Formants

Harmonics contained in a sound that often define the quality of that sound.

GM or General MIDI

An attempt to standardise MIDI file play back so that a song created on one sequencer will play back exactly on another, using the same sounds and effects. GM is often available as a 'mode' on a synthesiser, and like most standards, there are various variations and additions, such as GS and XG.

Hard disk recording

The term used to describe recording using a computer through an audio interface to a computer hard disk drive.

Headroom

The difference between an input signal and the maximum signal an audio system can take without distorting.

Hertz

Unit for measuring frequency. It describes the oscillations per second.

Hyperdraw and Hyper editor

Hyper in Logic Pro parlance means visual editing of controller and other MIDI events.

Instrument

In Logic Pro, an instrument is a representation of a patch or sound on a MIDI device. You use an instrument to record or play back MIDI data. They are defined within the Environment window. It's also used to refer to Virtual instrument plug-ins.

Key commands

Most of Logic Pro's parameters can have a Key command assigned to them, if you prefer not to use menus and on screen buttons. Some of Logic Pro's parameters only have Key commands.

Layer

In the Environment, a layer is a 'page' containing Environment objects. Its main function is to keep the Environment tidy and easy to use by grouping together related objects.

Mac

Apple's Macintosh computer.

Main volume

The volume of a MIDI device is adjusted by MIDI controller 7.

Meta event

These are events internal to Logic Pro, and are used to control various things, such as the automatic changing of Screensets.

Metronome

The 'click' you play along with in Logic Pro.

MIDI

MIDI stands for Musical Instrument Digital Interface. This was first established to allow the connection of two or more electronic musical instruments. This serial communication protocol has gone on to become the method of interfacing keyboards, computers and a wealth of MIDI devices and has become one of the most enduring 'standards' of modern times. MIDI data is also used when recording and playing back Virtual instrument plug-isn.

MIDI channel

MIDI devices send and receive data on up to 16 MIDI channels. these are not to be confused with the number of tracks a MIDI sequencer can record on which can, on modern computers, be almost infinite. Well a pretty large number anyway.

MIDI clock

A timing message embedded in the MIDI data enabling instruments such as drum machines to keep in time with another MIDI device, such as a sequencer.

MIDI controller

This is MIDI information used to control other MIDI parameters than notes themselves. Controllers can be used to adjust volume, pan, balance etc.

MIDI event

Any MIDI data recorded into Logic Pro is an Event.

MIDI file

a 'standard' song file designed to be universally playable on MIDI sequencers. There are three types of MIDI file.

For maximum portability, use Type 0, in Logic Pro. It's a good idea to normalize all sequence parameters prior to saving the song as a MIDI file.

MIDI interface

The hardware interface, containing the 5 pin DIN sockets that MIDI needs to communicate. These can come in many forms from the inbuilt MIDI IN and OUT on the Atari ST, through simple single port interfaces connected to a computer's USB ports, to complex multi channel interfaces allowing a sequencer to access more than 16 MIDI channels.

MIDI IN, MIDI OUT and MIDI THRU

These sockets are found on MIDI devices. MIDI IN and OUT are pretty self explanatory while MIDI THRU allows the MIDI data to pass through the device unaltered.

MIDI machine control (MMC)

MMC allows a sequence to control various parameters on some tape machines and other MIDI devices. You could, for example, use MMC to put a Fostex R8 8 track tape machine into record, and select the track to be recorded on.

MIDI message

The data passed between MIDI devices. MIDI messages can be note data, controller data, SysEx data and the like.

MIDI modes

MIDI modes determine how a MIDI device will respond to, or send out, MIDI data.

MIDI module

A sound generating, MIDI controlled device with no keyboard or other controller.

MIDI remote

You can assign many of Logic Pro's functions to an external MIDI device, so you could for example control Environment faders with a slider on your synthesiser, or put Logic Pro into play with an unused key on a keyboard.

MIDI time code

Unconfusingly, time code sent via MIDI. Most usefully used for converting SMPTE time code to a format that sequencers understand to keep them in sync with external devices such as tape and video machines.

Modifier keys

Keys on a computer keyboard, such as Control, Shift and Alt that modify the action of other keys.

Multi timbral

The ability of a synthesiser or module to produce several different sounds on different MIDI channels at the same time.

Normalize

See Fixing.

Object

Logic Pro is an 'object orientated' sequencer. What this means in practice is that everything is defined as an object – notes, sequences, MIDI modifiers, output ports etc. All the objects in Logic Pro have similar parameters, making it easy to move from one part of the program to another.

Parameter

In Logic Pro, objects can have parameters that can be changed. Often, these parameters are changed in a Parameter box.

Patch

On a MIDI device, a patch is a sound, or easily recallable set-up, for example, on a effects unit.

PC

An IBM type computer, usually running the Windows Operating System.

Plug-ins

These are software representations of Instruments or effects units that run under Logic Pro.

Program change

Program changes are MIDI events used to change patches on MIDI devices.

Quantize

Quantizing is 'bringing into time' unruly MIDI note data. It's used, for example, to bring drum parts into time. Quantizing can be used as a creative or restorative tool. It's non destructive within Logic Pro.

Quick swipe

Logic Pro's feature enabling the user to make rapid edits of multiple takes.

RAM

The memory in a computer where programs are run when they are loaded from hard disk RAM stores data temporarily and all data is lost when the computer is switched off.

Real time

This is the term for recording into a sequencer as if it was a tape machine, or for replaying controller data to control an external MIDI device. See Step time.

Region

Within Logic Pro, a sequence is a part recorded on a track in the Arrange window, or a section of an audio recording.

ROM

The permanent memory in a computer that runs essential operating software.

Sample rate

The number of times an analogue signal is measured per second in digital conversion.

Screensets

Within Logic Pro, a Screenset is a screen arrangement which can be stored and recalled.

SCSI

Small computer system interface. A fast communication system used for hard drives, CD ROMs etc.

Signal to noise ratio (S/N)

The ratio of signal level to noise level in an audio system expressed in dB.

SMPTE

A code, sounding not dissimilar to a modem or left field techno group, usually recorded on a video machine or tape recorder, and used to synchronise a sequencer with those devices.

Song

Logic Pro stores its sequences as Songs. When you are working in Logic Pro you are always in a Logic Pro song.

Soundcard

See Audio interface.

S/PDIF

Sony/Phillips Digital Interface. A low cost option digital interface. Similar to AS/EBU but using phono connectors.

Step time

Entering MIDI note data with the sequencer stopped, a note (or chord) at a time. See Real Time.

SysEx or System exclusive

A series of MIDI messages which enables different manufacturers to produce their own 'custom' MIDI data. SysEx is usually used to edit a synthesiser from a sequencer, or to store a whole memory dump from a MIDI device.

Toolbox

A toolbox, within Logic Pro, is a series of icons which, when selected, allows the mouse cursor to perform a different function. For example, select the pencil tool to draw MIDI data, the eraser tool to delete it.

Track

In Logic Pro, a track is where sequences are recorded in the Arrange page. A track always has an object assigned to it, most usually an instrument.

Transformer

An object that changes, or transforms, one type of MIDI data to another.

Transport

Logic's on screen representation of tape recorder style functions such as play, record etc.

Virtual instruments

These are DSP based representations of real instruments, such as samplers and synthesisers. Within Logic Pro, Virtual instruments are inserted as plug-ins on Audio objects and their parameters adjusted in the same way as more traditional plug-ins. Virtual Instruments use a lot of computer processing power.

Appendix 2
Logic and the internet

Logic is well represented on the Internet. There are mailing lists, web sites containing Environment set-ups and other useful files, along with other resources useful to the Logic user. As the Internet is a volatile area, with sites coming and going willy-nilly, all we are providing here is a pointer to the PC Publishing web site:

http://www.pc-publishing.com/logiclinks.html

At this address you will find links to other useful Logic sites and resources that will be updated as and when new information becomes available.

Index